Dance Nuggets

About the author: Clarke Fairbrother from Santa Ana, Ca.

While watching the second season of Dancing with the Stars, I noted that many of the competitors said: "**it was the hardest thing they had ever done, and it was the most rewarding**". I knew that ABC was not going to call me so I would have to find this experience on my own. On the internet I found a dance studio between work and home. I stopped by the studio and said "I would like to learn to dance". The receptionist summoned the owner of the studio immediately. The owner found a teacher to give me my first lesson that very day and then sold me the ten-lesson package.

A few months later a new instructor at the studio, Rachel, called me. She said I had two lessons left on my purchase and asked why I had not been in to the studio recently. I said that I guess I had not been inspired. She said "**come in and take a lesson from me and I will inspire you**". She treated the lessons like we were training for the Olympics. She assigned homework at the end of each lesson. She emphatically expected performance within my limitations and I have been taking lessons with her ever since.

A few months later, Rachel had me come in to "audition" to be in a studio "Dance Show", if I made the cut, though I am sure that everyone made it into the show. The show was to be presented in June of the next year, so I had six months to prepare. Soon thereafter Rachel and her partner, as New Zealand Latin Champions, were booked to be professionals on "Dancing with the Stars New Zealand" and she was going to be gone for several months. Rachel arranged for Melaina to be my substitute teacher in her absence to do my Boogie Woogie Bugle Boy show number. When Rachel returned, I had two instructors; Melaina for Smooth and Rachel for Latin, Rhythm and Night Club. The pictures on the back cover of the book are from shows and dance competitions that I did with Rachel and Melaina.

About the Book

This book contains information I have gleaned from my dance instructors, **Rachel White**, Just Dance OC or www.RachelRinaWhite.com, and **Melaina Brill**, Atomic Ballroom. I also received coaching from Danny Parker of Bumpin Ballroom. Put these names into your web browser to see all of the accomplishments of these wonderful dance instructors. Many of the concepts were explained to me hundreds of times before I assimilated them. The book also contains information that I have obtained from DIVIDA reference materials and videos.

The book first presents a few basics of dance and music that apply to all dances. The rest of the information is grouped by dance style as many of the dance styles have common movement basics. The first group is **American Smooth and International Standard**. The next major group is **American Rhythm and International Latin**. The last major group is the **Night Club Dances.** For each major style, the common elements of position and movement are presented. Before each style of dance there is a discussion of the elements that are unique to that dance style. **These are the best and most interesting parts of the book, pages 7-16 and 63-69**. The presentation order within each group is generally the order in which competitions run the dances. The last section of the book outlines sample dance routines. There is also **an index in the back that has the dances listed in alphabetical order**.

I compiled these nuggets of information for myself, a male dance student learning Bronze and Silver ballroom dances. Names and summaries of DIVIDA syllabus figures from 2019 for many dances are included. The summaries in this book leave out a lot of the detail that you will get from your dance instructor.

With the names of the figures from the summaries, you can put the **dance style and the name of the figure into an internet search engine, and often you will find a video that demonstrates the figure.** The **figure summaries are not easy reading**, but are to be used as an overview reference of the figures to jog your memory as to how it goes without having to go to a video.

Information in this book focuses on nuggets for the leader which I have put in **Bold**, so that they stand out. I hope this book will be a **useful reference** for your dance lessons. © Copyright February 3, 2019 Clarkef@newportpacific.com

Table of Contents

Dance in General	7
Music	7
Abbreviations	8
American Smooth and International Standard	9
Dance Positions and Movement	9
Waltz	16
Waltz Bronze American	17
Waltz-American Bronze Variations	19
Waltz-Silver American Syllabus	21
Waltz-International Bronze	26
Tango	29
Tango Bronze American Figures	30
Tango Bronze American Variations	32
Tango American Silver Figures	33
Tango – International Bronze Figures	35
Tango - International Silver	37
Foxtrot	39
Foxtrot Bronze American Variations	41
Foxtrot Silver American Figures	45
Foxtrot Bronze International	47
Foxtrot – International Silver	48
Viennese Waltz	51
Viennese Waltz American Bronze Figures	51
Viennese Waltz American Silver	53
Viennese Waltz -International	55
Quick Step	57
Quick Step Bronze Figures	57
Quick Step Silver Figures	58
Peabody	60
Rhythm and Latin	63
Cha Cha	67
Cha Cha Bronze American	70
Cha Cha Bronze Variations	72
International Cha Cha Cha Bronze	75
Rumba	78

American Rumba Bronze	78
Rumba Bronze Variations	80
International Rumba Bronze	84
International Rumba Silver Level	85
East Coast Swing	87
East Coast Swing Bronze	88
Jive Bronze	93
Jive Silver	94
Jive Gold	94
Bolero	96
Bolero Bronze Figures	96
Bronze Bolero Variations	97
Bolero Silver Figures	98
Mambo	101
Mambo Bronze Figures	102
Mambo Silver Figures	103
Samba	106
Samba Bronze American	106
Samba American Bronze Variations	107
Samba International Bronze	108
Samba International Silver	109
Paso Doble	111
Paso Doble Bronze	111
Paso Doble Silver	113
Night Club Dances	114
West Coast Swing	114
West Coast Swing Bronze	116
West Coast Swing Silver	118
West Coast Swing Alternate pushes and passes	119
West Coast Swing, other patterns	120
Salsa	121
Merengue	122
Merengue Bronze	122
Merengue Bronze Variations	124
Merengue Silver	124
Bachata	127

Bachata Figures	127
Hustle	129
Hustle Bronze Figures	129
Hustle Variations or Combinations	131
Night Club Two Step	132
Night Club Two Step Bronze	132
Night Club Two Step Silver	134
Country Two Step – Bronze	136
Country Two Step – Silver	137
Polka Bronze	138
Argentine Tango	139
Dance Routines	141

Dance in General

Dance is the expression of music through movement of the body. This expression starts with the movement of the feet to the beat of the music. The first few dance lessons are only about moving the feet to the right place at the right time. Gradually more body parts are added to the movement. The dancers winning dance competitions are **stretching the movements through the entire body to create constant movements** with the music and appropriate to the specific dance and the music.

The magic of ballroom dancing is the coordinated movements of the dance partnership. **The partnership is able to move in ways that are only possible with the combined efforts of the partners providing energy to each other.**

Music

Music is the guide for the dance movement and the coordination of the movements of the partnership. Most of the music we use for dance is 4/4 timing, four main beats (the underlying base beat) of music to a measure. The first beat of a measure is the biggest down beat. A down beat is note that is lower than the previous note, the second beat is normally up, the third beat is down and the fourth beat is up. There is commonly a noticeable sound, syncopation, between the third and fourth beat. Music commonly contains two or more measures to the phrase. The down beat of the five, the beginning of the second measure, is not as dramatic as the one. You can count the music as 1 2 3 4 twice or 1 2 3 4 5 6 7 8. Remember another 1 comes right after 8. The good dancers are always counting the music in their head as they dance. You have to plan where you are going next and count the music. Doing two things at once is hard for the male brain!

When starting dance movement from a stopped position the objective is to be moving on the first beat, being able to hear the previous three and four will allow you to prepare to be moving on the one.

Many dances use slows and quicks to define the timing for the movements. A slow (S) is two beats of music. A quick (Q) is one beat of music. Some dances, such as Cha Cha, use the syncopations (½ beats) between the main beats to define the timing for movements (movements are not always weight changes or steps). The half beat is counted as an "&". Some dances, such as Swing and Samba, use a ¼ beat in the timing. The ¼ beat is referred to as an "a", pronounced "ah".

Waltz is danced to music with ¾ timing. There are three beats to a measure, not four. The first beat is down followed by the rise of two and three. When you look at Waltz being danced, you will see that it uses the greatest amount of rise and fall in its movements to follow the lead of the music.

Abbreviations

The following are Abbreviations for often repeated words or phrases used in this book:

B Ball of the foot only
BF Ball of the foot changing to a flat foot
CBM Contra Body Movement
CBMP Contra Body Movement Position
CP Closed position
OP outside partner position
PP Promenade position
RSL Right side lead
LSL Left side lead
HT Heel toe foot placement
T Toe foot placement
TH Toe heel foot placement
BF Ball flat foot placement

F Facing
LOD Line of Dance
C Center (¼ turn to the left from LOD)
W Wall (¼ turn to the right from LOD)
DC Diagonal Center (1/8 turn to the left from LOD)
DW Diagonal Wall (1/8 turn to the right from LOD)

Q Quick, one beat of music
S Slow, two beats of music

FSB Forward side back
BSF Back side forward
UAT Under arm turn
ISUAT Inside under arm turn
OSUAT Outside under arm turn

American Smooth and International Standard

Smooth and Standard dances are **progressive dances** that move the couple mostly forward in a counter clockwise direction around the dance floor. This is line of dance, LOD. Movement often starts out forward along LOD or Diagonal Center, 1/8 turned to the left, or Diagonal Wall, 1/8 turned to the right. The direction, Center is ¼ turn to the left and the direction; Wall is ¼ turn to the right. Using these directions for the figures will allow the figures to flow together naturally. These starting directions for the figures will also be follower's first indication of what will come next.

Dancers moving very fast, by taking long graceful strides, are given priority on the outside edge of the dance floor. Slower dancers, using smaller strides or executing figures that do not progress, should be towards the center of the floor. The description of the figures in these sections gives beginning and ending alignments in the room as well as the dance holds used. When putting together a sequence of figures, the new figure must match the end position of the preceding figure. Basic steps are commonly used to link the figures together properly.

Dance Positions and Movement

Posture
Both partners are upright with spines lengthened up through the crown of the head with shoulder blades down, shoulders wide and the spine as straight as possible. Weight is aligned over **the ball of the foot** (specifically in the area behind the big toe) of the standing leg (the leg bearing most of the weight). The head, or sternum, should be over the standing leg, **nose over toes.** Both partners should be looking up slightly and left, over partner's shoulder. Followers should have a fully stretched spine, angled slightly leftwards, without tipping the shoulders. For both, this can best be accomplished by lifting rib cage up and bringing the bottom of the ribcage forward but only as far as to get the spine as straight as possible. The core, just below the rib cage, needs to be pulled back to keep the spine straight to prevent arching of the back. The bottom of the pelvis should be pulled forward to create a straight spine. The knees should be flexed. These opposing forces and positions create tone in the body that actually helps execute the movements. The tone also assists in maintaining balance. **As one part of the body moves one direction another part of the body must move the opposite direction to maintain balance.**

Focusing on carrying weight on **the inside part of the ball of the foot** will provide better balance as the outside of the foot is then available if needed for balance. If you are already on the outside part of the foot, there is nothing to stop you from tipping over when your balance is challenged.

As a little aside on the importance of this positioning of weight on the foot, I had a problem with my left big toe that caused me to use the outside of the left foot. Using the outside of the left foot in turn put most of the weight in on the inside edge of my left knee. I am quite sure that this weighting led to the need for a knee replacement for the inside of my left knee. **I think proper weight placement on the foot will maintain balanced weight placement in the knee and the knee will last a lot longer.**

Good posture on and off the dance floor will give you a confident, healthy look. Good posture will also make you look younger.

Partnership Dance Positions and Frame

Closed position

This is the most common position in the smooth dances. Taking closed dance position starts with the partners standing a couple of feet apart. Using good posture, the man raises his elbows up directly out to each side to a height slightly lower that his shoulders. From this position, he raises his left forearm up and towards his partner at about the woman's eye height. The follower moves toward the leader to take his left hand with her right with the palm facing forward and the thumbs crossed, partner's fingers held between his thumb and index finger. Hands should be equidistance between the partners at follower's eye height.

The woman moves toward the man placing left hand high on the man's arm close to the shoulder. This position will vary depending on the relative height of the partners. This positioning sets the separation of the partners from a few inches apart to lightly touching right front to right front of the torsos. The man's right hand is placed firmly on partner's back just below the left shoulder blade. The hand will be held flat with the fingers and thumb together. Partner rests her left arm lightly on the man's right arm with her fingers close to his shoulder and her wrist on his upper arm. The leader should keep his right elbow raised to maintain contact with follower's entire forearm. Legs should always be flexed at the knees.

In closed position, follower stands slightly to the leader's right so that on his forward steps, his left foot is outside of her right leg and his right foot is pointed between her feet pointed directly down the line of dance. The knees are flexed (softened), and in close contact position, partners thighs will be in contact with each other. Movements can be lead from legs and hips. Forward steps with leader's right leg will go between follower's legs. Both partners keep their head to the left looking over partner's right shoulder. **The partners maintain a bit of a "pull" connection between them so that follower can feel the movement of the leader's body as indicator of when and how much to move**.

Right outside partner position
To go to right outside position from closed position, both partners make a 1/8 turn to the left while maintaining their usual dance hold. This rotation places the follower strongly to the leader's right so that the right shoulders are opposite each other, but still parallel to partner. Forward steps by the leader are taken outside follower's right side.

Left outside partner position
To go to left outside position from closed position, both partners make a 1/8 turn to the left while maintaining their usual dance hold. This rotation places the follower strongly to the leader's left so that the left shoulders are opposite each other, but still parallel to partner. Forward steps by the leader are taken outside follower's left side. The couple can also get to left outside partner position from right outside partner position by making a quarter turn right as man steps forward with his right foot outside his partner.

Promenade
In promenade position the man's right hip and the ladies left hip are in contact or nearly in contact and the opposite sides of the bodies open out to form a V. The leader is very ahead of the follower in this position. The feet remain facing line of dance while the position is created by a **big rotation** of the upper body and hips towards follower, not by pushing with the arms. The follower's head will change position from looking left to looking right, down the line of dance. This transition is made with a twinkle figure in Waltz and Foxtrot (see figures in the various dances). In some dances it is done as a change within the hold without a transition figure.

There are many other relative positions used that will be discussed as the figures and dances that used them are discussed.

Movement in Standard and Smooth

The short description of movement in Smooth is "**Bend and Send**" which is used in waltz, foxtrot, tango and quickstep. Steps inside partner (basic hold) should have shoulder width or wider tracks. Steps outside partner will have narrow tracks with CBMP.

Forward: As the leg swings forward, keep the heel in contact with the floor. As weight is taken onto the moving foot, roll from the heel to the front of the foot. Forward movement is led from the knee. Keep the top of the body back as the leg swings forward by lowering on the standing leg. "**Stay back to go forward**".

Side: As the leg swings to the side, keep the inside edge of the ball of the foot in contact with the floor. Keep the top back as the foot moves to the side. Side steps can use sway, described below.

Backward: As the moving leg swings back in a straight line from the hip, keep the toe in contact with the floor. As weight is taken onto the moving foot, roll from the toe to the heel and release the toes of the front foot (the foot you are moving off of). Backward movement is led from the hip, like you are backing up to sit on a bar stool. Keep the top of the body forward as the leg swings back. "**Stay forward to go back.**"

Advanced description of movement in Smooth

The starting position for movement is the weight on one leg, with the foot, knee, hip and sternum in a straight line. The other foot will have the heal raised and the hip will be lifted. You should think of this as the neutral position for all dances. Try to begin and **end** each measure in this position. Releasing the hip of the standing leg will provide power to create faster foot movement. Learning to end each movement in this position takes a lot of practice, think of it as "leaving a little gas in the tank" to start the next movement. This is one of the biggest nuggets in the book.

The knees will be slightly bent (soft). Initiate forward movement from the standing leg at the start of each measure to create powerful strides. There is a small lowering in standing leg. Then the knee of the moving leg moves first, then the foot, then the hip and finally the top. The heel of the moving leg slides along the floor extending the split position. **Keep the heel of the standing (driving) leg on the floor as long as possible to create a powerful push.** As soon as weight is on the new standing leg (the sternum over the ball of the foot), that leg is used **to pull in** the other leg and **move it out into position for the next step.** This **movement is called a heel lead** and weight does arrive on the heel first, however **the weight should be moved to the ball of the standing leg** very soon thereafter. The good dancers **extend the time spent in the split weight position** and minimize the time spent with the weight mostly on one leg; this creates an image of constant motion as if the dancers were gliding on wheels. This is called body flight. **The spine is kept moving by rolling the weight through the foot (back** to front or front to back) of the standing leg and moving the pelvis forward or back to create a continuous movement of the body while on the standing leg. The good dancers **also use heavy foot pressure** on the non-standing leg to maintain balance and smooth motion. They also use tone in the inner thighs to keep the knees and thighs close to partner's knees and thighs as the leg moves under partner or beside partner. **Rise and fall should occur after the weight has been transferred to the new standing leg**, not during the movement from leg to leg.

When we start to learn Waltz, we bring the feet together at the end of the measure and use that position as the start of the next figure. The advanced dancers **end each step with the leg for the next step extended** in the direction of the next movement. Using this method will make quicker movement possible and it will assist you, almost require you, stay back to go forward and stay forward to go back. Remembering to extend the foot the takes a lot of practice. In smooth you do not need to have your weight squarely over the new standing leg exactly on the beat, being in the process go getting to the new standing leg will be fine.

The tracks for the steps in closed position should be kept wide, shoulder width or greater. Sometimes think of taking the step to be under the elbow. Narrow tracks are use when in outside partner position and in CBMP. The rotation for the CBMP of the top should come from the core, not the shoulders or arms. Taking steps using CBMP will make the steps more of a side step in which **sway** can be added.

Sway

Sway is the swing of the hips and lower ribcage in the movement in a side step or a turn. With side steps, sway is the willowy action of moving first the foot, the knee, then the hips, then the core and then the top of the body. In turns, sway is the inclination of the turn that is used to stop the previous momentum. Sway is initiated be moving the knee and hip of the standing leg towards the other leg causing the hip to rise. **This rising hip is the foundation of the inclination** of the upper body created by the sway. Do not to bend at the waist. The head inclines with the body. **The proper changes of inclination of the body in the movements create beautiful three-dimensional shapes** that will make you look great on the dance floor.

If you have taken the first step of a turning figure with your right foot, you will sway your hip to the left, creating an inclination of the upper body to the right, on the following two steps. If you have taken the first step of a figure turning left with your left foot, you will sway your hips to the right, creating an inclination of the upper body to the left on the following two steps. Said another way, the sway of the hips is to the outside of the turn creating an inclination of the top to the inside of the turn, i.e., banking into the turn. The sway helps to absorb the momentum created from the forceful first step. Sway also creates shapes that give the movement three dimensions. These three-dimensional movements can **be emphasized in the partnership with an expansion and subsequent contraction within the frame**, which will give the follower even greater three-dimension movement. Smooth proximity can also be very useful in creating shapes.

Turning

Turn is created by rotation within the standing leg <u>from the ankle through the hip</u>. Keep the sternum over the standing leg then move the sternum to the new standing leg. **To get more rotation than you can get from within the standing leg, place the foot that is to be the standing leg for the turn angled in the direction of the turn. This sort of foot windup needs to be anticipated when stepping on to the leg that will be creating the turn. <u>This is called an "Ugly Foot"</u>,** since normal, pretty feet, are aimed in the line of dance.

If the turn requires more rotation than can be created from the turning of the foot and leg, the momentum from the turning action is continued by the ball of the foot rotating on the floor. Additional momentum can be gained for a turn or spin from winding up of the top (from the core) in advance of the turn to be released to assist with rotation at the end of the turn. Think about moving the top in the direction of the turn as well as the feet. **The free arm should be up at shoulder height or higher and be used <u>as part of the wind up and release to create additional momentum</u>**. Using the arm in this way is natural and will assist in making the turn look effortless as well as coordinating the movement of the arm into the movement of the body.

<u>When going backwards in rotation, the bottom (the feet to the hips) goes first. When going forward in rotation, the top (sternum to belly bottom) goes first</u>. Left turning figures normally will have a left side lead in preparation for the turn. Right turning figures normally will have a right-side lead in preparation for the turn. When "in CBMP" (Contra Body Movement or Position) is listed in the figure, the side leads will be opposite i.e., left foot forward in CBMP would mean that the right hip through shoulder would be ahead of the left with the left foot going forward, creating a **windup in the core. The top of the body is rotated from the core, not the arms or shoulders.**

Leading

The leader must direct his partner's next movement, often with a rotation of the upper body, before changing his weight to the new foot. The short description of this concept is **"Create and Delay"**. There must always be a slight push or pull connection between the partners allowing the leader's small movements to be felt be the follower. In the closed hold that is a pull connection between the man's right hand and the follower's back that allows the follower to know whether the next movement is forward, back, side or turning. To begin forward movement, the man stands tall on the **balls of his feet** inclining the upper body forward slightly. He then lowers on the standing leg and sends his foot toward his partner keeping the hips and upper body over the sending supporting leg until the moving foot has established its position to receive weight.

Under arm turns are led by raising the left hand to a level slightly above partner's head and changing the hand position to a palm-to-palm position. If partner's turn is to her right from a closed position (an outside turn) the lead will be slightly right side of the partner. If partner's turn is to her left from a closed position (an inside turn) the lead will be going left towards partner's center. This is sometimes called a "Wipe the Nose" lead. Partner should hold her arm firmly in front of her face with the hand just above her head so that she can feel the speed in which the turn is led. Some partners like a bit of lead through the turn, others just like to get the signal and go on their own. Be sure to bring the lead arm down at the end of the turn to indicate the end of the turn, leaving the hand up indicates that more than one turn is expected. Leading a free spin for partner is similar, but the leading hand is only at waist level with a little push off the hand to start the turn.

Following

When watching couples dancing, notice that the follower always steps slightly after the leader begins to move. This delay produces a slight resistance and resulting pressure that is essential to good leading and following. Create and delay was referenced in leading. The leader moves first to lead and the delaying the movement until the follower has started to move, sometimes to stay out of the way. Sometimes the leader must follow, such as when leading a spin. The leader must pick up the connection with the follower where ever she ends up, as she is very busy turning.

In the outline of the figures, instructions for rotation are sometimes inserted between the steps as rotation often is started at the end of one step and completed at the beginning of the next step.

Waltz

Waltz is characterized by rise & fall and sway. The feet stay in contact with the floor while moving creating a smooth, gliding look. Waltz has an elegant gracefulness with a romantic feel. Tempo is generally 30-32 measures per minute. The basic timing is 1 2 3, following music that has three beats per measure.

Footwork

Moving forward, the first step the weight lands on the heel first then rolls onto the toe, the second step is on to the toe, staying on the toe, the third step starts on the toe and transitions onto the heel.

Moving backward, the first step the weight lands on the toe first then rolls to the heel, the second step is on to the toe, staying on the toe, the third step starts on the toe and transition onto the heel.

Chasses, with timing of 1 2 & 3 moving forward, are heel toe, toe, toe, toe heel. Chasses moving backward are toe heel, toe, toe, toe heel.

Rise & Fall

Rise from the beginning position, with the knees slight bent, can come from the knee and or the foot. The **knees should never reach a fully straightened position**, just a change in the bend of the knees. Rise should be smooth, gradual and high onto the toes. There is no rise on back steps on count 1, only commencement of body rise. Rise begins at the end of 1 (no foot rise on back steps), continues to rise on 2 3. Lowering back down occurs at the end of 3. Rise and fall should occur after the weight has been transferred to the new standing leg, not during the movement from leg to leg. Transfer of weight is completed when the sternum is centered over the ball of the foot.

The 3 is the busiest part of the rise and fall. Breaking the count into four parts, the actions (3 e & a) are: 3 continue to rise to the highest, e' lower to the heel of the standing leg, & compress into the knees bringing the thighs forward, a' release of the free leg to the new direction.

The more advanced dancers incorporate sway into the movement. See the discussion on sway in the previous section. **Swing, sway and rise** become the order of operations when a proper sway is used. Swing out the leg on 1, sway on 2 (sway does create some rise and some amount of turn will need to be included in the second step as sway is only used with side steps or turns) and rise and then lower on 3.

Waltz Bronze American

All figures have 1 2 3 timing, closing feet on 3 unless noted. Closing the feet means to bring the feet together and change weight.

1A. Box Step (Straight) begins and ends in closed position.
The first ½ of the box step or basic is left foot forward then the right foot to the side and slightly forward completing with the left foot closing to right foot changing weight to the left foot so that the right foot is prepared to move.
Second ½ of the box step is right foot back, left foot side and slightly back, right foot closes to left foot changing weight.
1B. Box with Underarm Turn begins with a forward ½ box, on the back ½ of box lead follower's turn off to the left side, then a forward ½ box to complete follower's turn, and the back ½ of box to closed position
2. Progressive basic is a series of box steps, generally moving forward.
3A. Left Turning Box is a series of box steps turning to the left. Amount of rotation can vary from 1/8 to 3/8 per measure with ¼ being common. Left turn box is started with a left foot forward step.
3B. Right Turning Box is a series of box steps turning to the right. Amount of rotation can vary from 1/8 to 3/8 per measure with ¼ being common. Right turning box is started with a left foot back step.
4A. Balance Steps: Forward & Back or Side to Side start facing line of dance, 1 step forward then hold 2 3. This is called Hesitation timing. Same timing is used going to the back or side.
4B. Balance and Box begins facing line of dance and ends facing center. Figure starts with a balance step forward, 1 hold 2 3, followed by back side close (the back half of a basic with a ¼ turn to the left). Figure can be used for turning in tight places, much like a Foxtrot left rock turn. *An underarm turn or spin turn can be added to the back half of the figure.*
5. Simple Twinkle is used to get to promenade position or from promenade position to closed position.
Twinkle open begins facing wall or diagonal wall in closed position.
Left foot forward, right foot side and slightly forward with 1/8 turn to left, left foot closes to right foot turning frame into promenade position facing line of dance. You can add a little dipping action to this transition.
Twinkle close is used to get from promenade position to closed position.

Right foot forward and across in CBMP commencing turn to the right, 1/8 turn right, left foot side, right foot closes to left foot. Figure ends facing wall or diagonal wall. You can add a little dipping action to this transition.

6. Two-Way Underarm Turn begins facing line of dance and ends facing wall.
Measure 1 is a forward ½ of box,
Measure 2 is a back ½ of box leading partner to an outside under arm turn off to the left side,
Measure 3 is a twinkle forward from closed position to offset position & leading partner to step forward and side into opposing stretch positions,
Measure 4 twinkle from offset right position to left side position lead under arm turn (forward, side, together and turn),
Measure 5 is a twinkle from closed position to promenade position collecting partner,
Measure 6 is a twinkle close from promenade position to closed position. Figure can be used without the first two measures to end Face to Face, Back-to-back.

7. Face to Face - Back-to-back begins facing line of dance and ends facing center
Measure 1 is a forward half box,
Measure 2 is a back half of box with an underarm turn,
Measure 3 is a twinkle from closed position to face to face (FF),
Measure 4 is a twinkle for FF to back-to-back (BB),
Measure 5 is a twinkle from BB to BB to promenade position,
Measure 6 is a twinkle from promenade position to closed position.
An under arm turn or spin can be added on any of the forward movements.

8. Reverse Turn begins facing diagonal center and ends facing diagonal wall in closed position
Measure 1 is forward, side turning to the left 3/8, close,
Measure 2 is back, side turning to the left 3/8, close.
Use a left side lead in left turning figures.
An under-arm turn can be added on the back half of the figure

9. Natural Turn begins facing diagonal wall ends facing diagonal center closed position
Measure 1 is forward, side turning to the right 3/8, close,
Measure 2 is back, side turning to the right 3/8, close.
Use a right-side lead in right turning figures.
An under-arm turn can be added on the back half of the figure

10. Progressive Twinkles begins facing line of dance outside partner position with turns on the 3, in either closed position or two hand open position.
Measure 1 is a twinkle from closed position to right outside partner.
Measure 2 is a twinkle from right outside partner to left outside partner position.
Measure 3 is a twinkle from left outside partner to right outside partner.
Measure 4 is a twinkle from right outside partner to closed position.

11. Turning Twinkles begins facing the wall with a twinkle from closed to promenade position, forward in promenade position on 1, 180 turn on 2 left-to-right hand hold, close feet on 3, forward along line of dance, 180 turn to promenade position on 2, close feet on 3, twinkle close.

12. Grapevine begins facing diagonal wall in closed position. Move forward on 1, forward pivoting 90 to the right on 2, back passing feet on 3, back on 4, side on 5, close on 6. Figure ends diagonal wall in closed position.

13. Promenade Chassé begins facing diagonal wall in promenade position with inside foot free. Forward **1 2 & 3** in promenade position. On the & count, the right foot closes to the left, all on the toes. End with twinkle ending or another promenade figure.

Chassé, French for 'to chase', is a dance term used in many dances in many variations. All variations are triple-step patterns of gliding character in a "step-together-step" pattern. The word comes from ballet terminology.

14. Fallaway and Box begins facing diagonal center in closed position.
Measure 1 is a twinkle from closed position to Fallaway position which is promenade position backing line of dance,
Measure 2 is a fallaway in promenade position, back 1, back 2 and a slip pivot on 3 (step back & off the track to closed position)
Measure 3 is a forward half of under turned left turning box in closed position,
Measure 4 is a back half of under turned left turning box in closed position.
Figure ends facing diagonal center.

15. Twinkle & Weave begins facing diagonal wall in closed position.
Measure 1 is a twinkle from closed position to promenade position.
Measure 2 is a weave from promenade position turning left on 2 to right outside partner. This action should create a nice whoosh.
Measure 3 is a back (use ugly foot) twinkle turning right from right outside partner to promenade position. This action should create a nice whoosh.
Measure 4 is a twinkle close from promenade position to closed position.
Figure ends facing diagonal wall.

Choreography notes – An under-arm turn can be led anytime partner has a side step. Any figure that can be led in a straight line can be led in a curve or circle.

Waltz-American Bronze Variations

In general, when adapting figures from Foxtrot SSQQ to Waltz, use a hesitation step for the first slow and finish the SQQ as 123.

1. Single Corté (Tango) begins in closed position facing line of dance.

Start with two forward basics, step back with left foot leaving right foot forward & hold 2 3 (Hesitation timing), replace weight to right foot, left foot side, close right foot to left foot changing weight turn ¼ turn right to end facing wall in closed position.

2. Open Fan (Tango) begins in closed position facing wall, twinkle open, promenade check to bring partner side-by-side left-to-right hand hold, left foot for then ¼ turn right towards partner on 1 and point right foot to right on 2 hold 3, turn ¼ right bring right foot across and through, side together for a twinkle close.

3. Continuous Left Rock Turn (Tango) starts in closed position facing line of dance. Move forward using ½ box with ¼ turn to the left, middle measure is a rocking turn left holding the legs in CBMP which means leave the legs in rocking position, steps go back and off the track turning left, rock forward on the right, rock back on the left, 270 turn on the rocks, then a forward ½ box to finish. Figure ends in closed position facing line of dance after total 360 turn over the three measures. Add ¼ turn on the 2nd forward ½ box if you want to finish end facing center. Turns going backwards start turning from the feet, not the top.

4A. Fifth Position Breaks (V. Waltz) starts in closed position facing line of dance. 5th position break to left (left foot side, right foot behind left foot, replace weight on left foot), 5th position break to the R, end with for ½ box turning to face diagonal center.

4B. Fifth Position Breaks with Underarm Turn (V. Waltz) begins in closed position facing line of dance. 5th position break to left, open break to right (like 5th position only step back a bit more, open right arm), 5th position break to the left leading under arm turn for partner, 5th position break to the right ending in closed position, forward ½ box turn 1/8 left to end facing diagonal center.

5A. Cross Body Lead (V. Waltz) begins in closed position facing line of dance. Balance step (forward and hold, hesitation), left foot back and off the track, right foot side leading partner across, making a 180 turn with the three steps, forward ½ box to finish. Ends facing line of dance

5B. Cross Body Lead with Underarm Turn (V. Waltz) begins in closed position facing line of dance. Balance step (forward and hold, hesitation), left foot back and off the track leading under arm turn for partner, right foot side leading partner across, making a 180 turn with the three steps, forward ½ box to finish. Figure ends facing line of dance.

6. Promenade (Foxtrot) begins in promenade position facing line of dance. Left foot forward in promenade position with hesitation timing on the first step and 1 2 3 to finish, twinkle close. Figure ends in closed position facing wall.

7. Zig Zag outside Partner (Foxtrot) begins in closed position facing diagonal wall. Left foot forward in closed position with hesitation timing going right outside partner, right foot forward, left foot side turning ¼ turn to the right, right foot closes to left in closed position, left foot back in closed position with hesitation timing going to left outside partner position, right foot back, left foot side turning ¼ turn to the L, right foot closes to left. Figure ends in closed position facing diagonal wall.

8. Turning Twinkle to Outside Partner (Foxtrot) begins in closed position facing line of dance. Twinkle open to promenade position, forward, side, close turning partner to right outside partner, hesitation step backwards, twinkle close to closed position facing wall.

9. Promenade Twist (Foxtrot) begins in closed position facing line of dance. Twinkle open to promenade position moving center, right foot forward and across in CBMP twist 90 to left with partner running around 1 2 and pivoting on 3, left foot brushes to right foot no pressure, hesitation left foot forward right foot brushes left foot no pressure, right foot back, left foot side, right foot close for twinkle close. Ends closed position facing diagonal wall.

10. Promenade Pivot (Foxtrot) starts in promenade position moving line of dance. Left foot side (forward in promenade position) hesitation timing, right foot forward and across partner pivoting 180 to the right to cut off partner, left foot back "ugly foot" off the track pivoting 90 or 180, right foot forward in promenade position, hesitation timing line of dance, left foot forward, right foot side, left foot close to right foot for a twinkle close. Ends closed position facing wall of new line of dance or line of dance.

Waltz-Silver American Syllabus

For Silver American Waltz figures, **brush and pass the feet extending the leg for the next step instead of closing the feet** on 2 3 as is done in the Bronze figures. Timing is 1 2 3 unless otherwise noted.

Many of the figures start and end with a twinkle open and twinkle close. Successive promenade position figures may be danced between the open twinkle and the closed twinkle.

1. Open Left Box begins in a closed position facing diagonal center.
Measure 1 is a 3/8 left turn on the forward step, then step to the side, then a back step in CBMP (FSB).
Measure 2 is a 3/8 left turn on the back step, then step to the side, then a forward step in CBMP (BSF).
The figure ends facing diagonal wall in left outside partner position.

2. Open Right Turn begins in closed position facing diagonal wall.
Measure 1 is a **twinkle from closed position to promenade position**. The **silver twinkle** begins facing wall or diagonal wall in closed position.

Left foot forward, right foot forward with 1/8 turn to left for leader into promenade position, left foot forward in promenade position in line of dance or diagonal wall depending on the next figure. In the open right turn the goal is line of dance.
Measure 2 is a right turn from promenade position to right outside partner.
Measure 3 is a heel turn (Impetus) from right outside partner to promenade position.
Measure 4 is a continuity ending (starts in promenade position and ends right outside partner) or start a new figure that starts in promenade position. Figure ends facing diagonal center.

3. Open Right Turn with Underarm Turn starts in closed position facing diagonal wall.
Measure 1 is a twinkle from closed position to promenade position.
Measure 2 is a right turn from promenade position to right outside partner (same as figure 2 up to here).
Measure 3 is a chasse to the right 12&3 with under arm turn.
This could also be a free spin.
Figure ends in open facing position facing diagonal center.

4. Twinkle Connection begins facing diagonal center while moving along the line of dance in open facing position (which is the ending position of figure 3, an under arm turn or a free spin).
Step 1 is right foot forward and across in CBMP to outside partner's left,
Step 2 is left foot forward between partner's feet while rotating upper body to the right and placing right hand on follower's shoulder blade,
Step 3 is a step to the side in promenade position. The figure ends in promenade position face diagonal center.

5. Check & Developé begins in open left outside position in double hand hold facing diagonal center.
Measure 1 move the left foot forward and across in CBMP for a check in left outside open partner position while raising hands to lead follower's Developé, which is to lean back while raising the left leg almost to leader's armpit. The position is held for 2 3. When using a checking action, left foot can be turned out for stability.
Measure 2 move right foot back in CBMP, move left foot to the side rotating the top to the left 180 and brushing the right foot to the left, then right foot back.
Measure 3 move the left foot back in CBMP, move the right foot to the left foot making a heal turn, an open impetus, collecting partner from two hand hold into promenade position and a forward step with the left in promenade position. Figure ends facing diagonal center.
An alternative measure 3 would be to lead a spin turn from the open position.

6. Chair & Slip begins in a closed position facing diagonal wall.
Measure 1 is a twinkle from closed position to promenade position.

Measure 2 is a promenade check (which is forward on the right), rocking back on the left (the chair), then right foot small step back & to the left depending on the rotation desired (slip pivot is just one step), ending in closed position. The foot can be turned out in the checking action.

7. Progressive Open Twinkles begin in closed position facing diagonal wall.
Measure 1 is a forward twinkle from closed position to right outside partner.
Measure 2 is a forward twinkle from right outside partner to left outside partner.
Measure 3 is a forward twinkle from left outside partner to right outside partner.
Measure 4 is a forward ½ of Viennese open right turn (see figure 12),
Measure 5 is back twinkle from right outside partner to left outside partner.
Measure 6 the back half of an open left box from left outside partner.

8A. Hairpin from Reverse begins in closed position facing diagonal center.
Measure 1 is a forward ½ of a left open box - forward, side, back in CBMP.
Measure 2 is back, side, forward in CBMP, curving run to right outside partner (Hairpin),
Measure 3 is back in CBPM, right foot closes to left for a heel turn from right outside partner to promenade position (open Impetus) and left foot forward in promenade position. Figure ends in promenade position facing diagonal center ready to move diagonal center.
An alternate Measure 3 is to do a chasse to the right (12&3) while leading partner for a turn or a spin.

8B. Hairpin - From Promenade Position begins in closed position facing diagonal wall.
Measure 1 is a twinkle from closed position to promenade position.
Measure 2 is a right foot forward and across in CBMP, left foot forward, right foot small step forward curving to right outside partner (Hairpin),
Measure 3 is left foot back in CBPM, right foot closes to left for a heel turn from right outside partner to promenade position (open Impetus) and left foot forward in promenade position. Figure ends in promenade position facing diagonal center, ready to move line of dance.
An alternate Measure 3 is to do a chasse to the right (12&3) while leading partner for a turn or a spin.

9. Fallaway & Weave begins in closed position facing diagonal center, Measure 1 is a syncopated 1&23 fallaway to right outside partner, left foot forward, right foot forward between partners legs rotating to the left 180 to open up the partnership into closed position right outside partner, left foot back in CBMP, right foot back.
Measure 2 is a syncopated 1&23 weave, left foot back in CBMP, right foot back, left foot side in CBMP rotating left 180, right foot forward ending in closed position right outside partner facing diagonal center.

10. Oversway begins in closed position facing diagonal wall. Twinkle from closed position to promenade position, step in promenade position into Challenge Line (step 1 hold 2 3) shape with rotation to the right, then, Oversway, no steps a lowering and rotation to the left, then Hover (change weight to the right on 1 beginning to rise, brush feet together on 2 continuing to rise and step out to the left on 3 lowering) to promenade position

11. Pivot from Promenade begins in closed position facing diagonal wall, Twinkle from closed position to promenade position. Step forward and to the right and pivot 180 in front of partner. Connect with partner right thigh to right thigh and continue 180 turn to the right. End with a heel turn closed position to promenade position (Open Impetus). Remember to **Ugly Foot** (over rotate the foot in the direction of the turn) especially on the turn going backwards. **Rotate the knee of the ugly foot leg in behind the knee of the standing leg to get more rotation.**

12. Syncopated Viennese Turn begins in closed position facing diagonal wall. *This figure is no longer in the silver syllabus.*
Measure 1 movement starts with a twinkle to promenade position,
Measure 2 is right foot forward and across in CBMP, left foot forward, right foot side rotating left, left crosses in front of right. Timing is 12&3.
Measure 3 is right foot back, left foot to the side, right foot closes to left, left foot to the side and slightly forward. Timing is 12&3.
Measure 4 is right foot forward and across, left foot to the side and forward, right foot forward in CBMP to right outside closed position.

13. Flip Flop outside positions begins in closed position facing diagonal wall.
Measure 1 starts with a twinkle to open promenade position opening out to a V position on step 3. *Maintain a pull connection with partner while opened out*.
Measure 2 leader makes a passing right turn from open promenade position to open counter promenade position in front of follower. *Step 2 of this measure is a good place to add sway*.
Measure 3 lead to follower make a passing right turn to the other side in front of leader while leader takes three small forward steps.
Measure 4 is a continuity ending to get to closed position.
Maintain good CBMP in this figure.
An alternative entrance into flip flops is from an open facing position at the end of an underarm turn or free spin or from Developé'. The continuity ending can be replaced with an entrance into pivots.

14. Check to Open Fallaway begins in a closed position facing diagonal wall.
This is similar to the face to face, back-to-back in bronze.
Measure 1 starts with a left turning twinkle from closed position to promenade position.

Measure 2 is a leader's promenade check to move partner ahead and to leader's left in single hand hold.

Measure 3 in single hand hold move left foot forward, right foot side to face partner, left foot crosses behind right.

Measure 4 is a moving of the right foot forward, lead partner to turn and make a two-step right turn.

Measure 5 is continuity ending in promenade position.

15. Alternating Underarm Combination begins in closed position facing diagonal wall. Start with a right turning twinkle to promenade position, then leaders under arm turn from promenade position to left side partner, left foot forward and chasse to right 12&3 for follower's syncopated outside under arm turn. The figure ends in open facing position. This figure can be followed by a figure 4.

16. Rounders' (non-syllabus) in CP, F DW into corner starts with a progressive basic, then four measures turning right, ends F DW NLOD. Figure turns 270.

Measure 1 is right foot forward rotating to the right for a side step with the left, then forward with the right. Steps are similar to a Boto Fogo in Samba.

Measure 2 is left foot forward rotating right, hook right foot behind left foot and then left foot to the side continuing to turn right.

Measure 3 repeats measure 1.

Measure 4 repeats measure 2.

17. Free turn (or Check) to Fallaway (modified form of Gold figure 9) starts CP F DW.

Measure 1 is a twinkle to promenade moving LOD.

Measure 2 is a leader's promenade check to move partner ahead and to leader's left in single hand hold both facing LOD. Steps are right foot forward and across leading partner to rollout to the left, replace the weight back to the left foot (the check) and side step to the right to create the one hand open position with both facing LOD.

Measure 3 (1&23) is 1 left foot forward, & right foot side to face partner (like in Face to Face Back-to-back), 2 is left foot to the side crossing behind right foot in CBMP, 3 is rotate on left foot to face line of dance and step forward on the right.

Measure 3 can be repeated varying arm styling from the first Measure 3.

Measure 4 can be a simple ending of a chasse to the right with free spin for partner. Gold syllabus ending is measure 4 is both turn ending facing LOD. Measure 5 is both partners turn to back LOD, ronde and slip pivot to closed position F DW.

18. Inside Under Arm Turn to Shadow begins with the first measure of an open left. Measure 2 step back and off the track while leading an inside UAT, maintain light contact with partner with the right hand during the turn to indicate intent to end in shadow position. Change hand hold to left to left hand hold at the end of the turn. Leader should end ahead in the movement. In this position the partnership commonly makes a two measure turn to the right with the partner on the inside of the turn making a small step off the track to accommodate partner on the outside of the turn. Forward steps in shadow alternating side leads can be added. Exit shadow by leading a spin out, perhaps into flip flops.

Waltz-International Bronze

All figures use closed position and 1 2 3 timing for unless otherwise noted.

1. Left foot Closed Change begins facing diagonal wall. Movement starts with left foot: forward, side, close.
2. Natural Turn begins facing diagonal wall. Movement starts with right foot: forward, side, close with a 3/8 turn to right.
3. Right Foot Closed Change begins facing diagonal center. Movement starting with right foot: forward, side, close
4. Reverse Turn begins facing diagonal center. Movement starts with left foot: forward, side, close with a 3/8 turn to the left.
5. Whisk begins facing diagonal wall, left foot forward, right foot side & forward, left foot closes behind right foot, in promenade position
6. Chassé from Promenade Position begins facing diagonal wall along line of dance in promenade position right foot forward, left foot forward, right foot close to left foot, left foot forward, 12&3 timing.
7. Natural Hesitation Change begins with a natural turn, 123, 4 left foot back beginning turn to the right, 3/8 turn to right, 5 right foot side (small step-heel pull), 6 left foot closes to right no weight.
8. Progressive Chases' to Right begins facing diagonal center, left foot beg turn to L, 1/8 turn, right foot side, 1/8 turn, left foot closes to right foot, right foot to side and slightly back, 12&3 timing.
9. Back Lock begins backing diagonal wall with 12&3 timing. Start with left foot back in CBMP, right foot back, left foot crosses in front of right foot, right foot diagonal back.
10. Closed Impetus begins backing line of dance, left foot back beg turn to R, 3/8 turn, right foot closes to left foot (heel turn), ¼ turn, left foot side and slightly back.
The International syllabus uses the term "impetus" in Waltz, Foxtrot or Quickstep to describe **a heel turn for the man turning to the right**. The open impetus is one of several ways to get into promenade position and is used to turn dancers around corners or change their direction on the dance floor. It is often used after a natural turn. The open impetus has less turn for the man than the closed impetus. The closed impetus remains in closed position, while the open impetus ends in promenade position.

11. Reverse Corté begins backing line of dance, right foot back beginning right 3/8 turn, left foot closes to right foot without weight, hold and lower on 3.

12. Back Whisk begins diagonal center along line of dance, left foot back in CBMP, right foot diagonal back, left foot crosses behind right foot in promenade position now facing diagonal wall.

13. Natural Spin Turn begins with the first measure same as natural turn to backing line of dance, 2nd Measure left foot back ½ turn to right, right foot held in CBMP (a pivot), right foot forward in CBMP continuing the right turn, 3/8 turn, left foot to the side and slightly back, Figure ends backing diagonal center. Amounts of turn can vary to create other alignments.

14. Reverse Pivot begins backing line of dance, right foot back in CBMP small step turning up to ½ turn to left, left foot held in CBMP. This figure is just an & count.

15. Double Reverse Spin begins facing line of dance. On 1 the left foot moves forward beginning 3/8 turn to the left, on 2& right foot moves to side, ½ turn, on 3 left foot closes to right foot without weight (Toe Pivot). Amount turn and directions may vary.

16. Basic Weave begins backing diagonal wall. On 1 right foot moves back body turning left, on 2 the left foot moves forward continue with 1/8 turn, on 3 right foot moves to the side with 1/8 turn, on 4 the left foot moves back in CBMP, on 5 right foot moves back beginning a ¼ turn, on 6 the left foot moves side and slightly forward, pointing diagonal wall

17. Outside Change begins backing diagonal center left foot back, right foot back begins left turn, ¼ turn left, left foot to side and slightly back.

Waltz International Silver

18. Weave from Promenade Position begins after a whisk, in promenade position facing diagonal center. In two measures, make a full turn to the left, FFBBBF. Figure ends facing diagonal center.

19. Open Impetus to Wing begins backing line of dance, left foot back and off the track, right foot closes to left foot for the heel turn, left foot diagonal forward with left side leading in promenade position, right foot forward in CBMP and promenade position, left foot begins to close to right foot while leading partner to walk around in front, left foot closes to right foot without weight.

A **Wing** is a transitional movement that repositions the follower to the leader's left side. Thus, while many dance figures can precede a Wing, only a reverse movement can follow a wing, such as a reverse turn, double reverse spin, Telemark, fallaway reverse, or drag hesitation. The Wing begins with a forward hesitation while leading the woman to take three forward steps to the man's left side. Thus, the next figure will begin in outside partner position, moving into a reverse turn

20. Closed Telemark begins facing diagonal center, left foot forward beginning a turn to left, right foot side turning 3/8 left, left foot side and slightly forward turning 3/8 left. Figure ends facing diagonal wall.

Telemarks are reverse turns where the follower does a heel turn as the leader travels around her. There are similar Telemarks in foxtrot and quickstep. The Closed Telemark ends in closed position and the Open Telemark ends in promenade position.

21. Turning Lock begins backing diagonal center, 1 & 2 3 timing, right foot back with right side lead, left foot crosses in front of right foot, right foot back and slightly right beginning turn to left, left foot side and slightly forward turning ¼ left. Figure ends facing diagonal wall.

22. Open Impetus with Cross Hesitation begins backing line of dance, **Open Impetus**: left foot back beginning turns to the right, right foot closes to left foot turning 3/8 to the right, left foot diagonal forward left side lead in promenade position.

Cross Hesitation: right foot forward in CBMP and promenade position, right foot forward in CBMP and promenade position, left foot closes to right foot without weight, position held while partner rolls into closed position like a tango close. A cross hesitation is used to bring partner from promenade position to closed position with an action like a tango close in American Tango.

23. Open Telemark to Wing begins diagonal center, Telemark to promenade position, hesitation to lead partner into wing position. Figure ends facing diagonal center.

24. Open Telemark to Cross Hesitation begins facing diagonal center, with a Telemark to promenade position, cross hesitation to closed position. Figure ends facing diagonal wall.

25. Drag Hesitation begins facing diagonal wall or diagonal center with left foot forward beginning to turn left, right foot side turning 1/4 left, left foot closes to right foot without weight outside partner with 1/8 turn left.

26. Outside Spin begins backing diagonal center against line of dance with left foot small step back turning right, right foot forward in CBMP outside partner turning right, left foot to side and back completing one turn over the three counts. Partner turns with forward close forward steps.

27. Open Impetus to Weave begins backing line of dance, taking three measures. Measure one is an open impetus, right foot back in CBMP, heal turn and right foot forward in promenade position. Measure two is left foot forward beginning to turn left, right foot side and slightly back turning ¼ turn left, and then left foot back in CBMP turning 1/8 left. Measure three is right foot back beginning turn to left outside partner, left foot side and slightly forward turning 3/8 turn to left closed position. Figure ends facing diagonal wall.

Tango

Tango is characterized by a close hold, **a low center of gravity** and **an emphasis on Contra Body Movement**. It is a more angular dance with an emphasis on stopping actions. The feet are picked up slightly and placed on the floor instead of skimming the floor as in the other Smooth dances. There is no rise and fall; dancers maintain soft bent knees throughout. Movement in Tango is stealthy, almost cat-like and has a staccato feel from the action of moving quickly and stopping quickly.

Footwork

In forward walks and walks in promenade position, the heel is the first part of the foot to contact the floor. In backward walks the contact starts with the ball first and then heel. In swiveling actions, the contact starts with the heel and then the ball. When dragging the foot in the contact starts with the inside edge of ball. An example is the last step of a Tango Close. With side steps, the inside edges of ball heel contact the floor first.

Frame

Leader's frame should be wide from elbow to elbow, maintaining width across both the back and the chest. The right arm is further around and lower on the follower's back than in the other Smooth dances. The left arm is bent at about a 90-degree angle, with left hand held closer in toward the leader's body and face. Follower's arms should be light and responsive in the leader's frame. The left hand is placed behind and below the leader's upper right arm.

Promenade

Create promenade position by rotating the body (not pushing with the arms), which would result in breaking your frame. Remember that rotation of the body can come from the ankles to the spine.

Movement

Movement should be sharp and staccato. The first quick should have more emphasis than the second quick. Engage muscles through the mid-section of the body for a strong bracing action while still keeping the arms, neck and head relaxed and free. Do not use rise and fall in Tango. Knees should be softly flexed, weight placed over the center of the foot, maintaining the same height throughout the dance. Walks generally curve to the left and are taken lifting the foot slightly off the floor and placing it in position.

Tango Bronze American Figures

1A. Basic Straight begins in closed position facing line of dance. The timing is SSQQS for two forward walks and tango close (left foot forward, right foot side, left foot almost closes to right foot without weight). Figure ends facing line of dance. Tango close is used at the end of many figures.

1B. Curving Basic begins in closed position facing line of dance. The timing is SSQQS two forward walks and tango close all curving to the left or the right.

2A. Promenade Turning Left begins in promenade position facing diagonal center, SS tap & turn then pull into closed and QQS to finish. Figure ends in closed position facing diagonal center.

2B. Promenade Turning Right begins in promenade position facing diagonal wall, SS, walk in promenade position forward with right foot pivot from promenade position to closed position, QQS, back tango close. Figure ends closed position facing center.

3A. Single Corté begins closed position facing line of dance, SS, back with left foot holding right in position creating a shape with partner and replace, QQS, tango close. Figure ends facing line of dance.

3B. Double Corté begins in closed position facing diagonal center, QQ, forward turning left, back completing the 180-left turn, SS, Corte and recover, QQ, forward turning left, back completing the 180-left turn, SS, Corté and recover, QQS, tango close. Figure ends facing line of dance.

4. Progressive Rocks begins in closed position facing line of dance, SS, two forward walks, QQS, left foot forward leaving right foot in position, rock back onto right foot, forward on left foot, QQS, right foot forward leaving left foot in place, rock back onto left foot, forward on right foot, QQS, tango close. xxx are the rocks. Figure ends facing line of dance.

5A. Open Fan begins in promenade position facing diagonal wall, SS 2 forward walks curving left, QQ&S, forward check release to left side partner flick, (left foot forward, right foot side, left foot brush tap to side), SS, open fan from closed position promenade position then lead follower to closed position (left foot diagonally forward swivel right leg points diagonally back, right foot forward and across in CBMP ends with left foot side without weight), QQS, tango close. Figure ends facing center.

5B. Open Fan with Underarm Turn begins in promenade position facing diagonal wall, SSQQ& S, open to fan as in 5A, SS, two walks curving left with an under arm turn for partner, QQS, tango slow from under arm turn to closed position. Figure ends facing center.

6. Running Steps begins in closed position facing line of dance; SSQQ, 3 forward steps and a side check, SSQQ, 3 forward steps and a side check, QQS tango close (right & slightly back on _). Figure ends facing line of dance.

7. Checked Promenade begins in promenade position facing diagonal wall moving line of dance, SQQS, 3 forward walks in promenade position the right foot forward check, S&S back on _ two back walks in Fallaway position. Figure ends promenade position B diagonal center.

8A. Reverse Turn begins in closed position facing diagonal center, QQS, forward half of reverse turn (left foot forward in CBMP, turn left ¼ turn, right foot side and slightly back, 1/8 left turn, left foot back in DBMP, QQS, back half of reverse turn (referred to as Closed Finish, FR back, 3/8 turn, left foot side and slightly forward, right foot closes to left foot slightly back). Figure ends closed position facing diagonal wall.

8B. Reverse Turn with Outside Swivel begins in closed position facing diagonal center, QQS, forward half of reverse turn, QQS, back half or reverse turn, SS follower's swivel from right outside partner to promenade position, lead pivot to closed position, QQS, tango close. Figure ends facing line of dance.

9. Right Side Fans begins in closed position facing diagonal center, QQSS, Forward half of Reverse turn to follower's outside swivel then pivot from promenade position to closed position, QQSS repeat, QQS tango close. Figure ends facing diagonal center.

10. Contra Rocks begin in closed position facing line of dance, QQS, Contra rocks and windup, QQS Pivot to left then 2 forward curving walks, QQS Contra rocks and windup, QQS back half of Reverse turn

11. Continuous Left Rock Turn begins in closed position facing diagonal wall, QQS Contra rocks windup, QQQQ turning rocks to ¼ turn left each rock, QQS back half of reverse turn, QQS Contra Rock to promenade position. Figure ends facing diagonal wall.

12. Twist Turn to the Right begins in promenade position facing diagonal wall moving line of dance, SQQS, 2 walks in promenade position then side & cross to prepare for twist, QQ Twist turn to left. Figure ends promenade position facing diagonal wall.

13. Check and Corté begins in closed position facing diagonal wall, QQSS, under turned forward half of Reverse turn to follower's outside check, recover to promenade position, QQSS, Promenade turning right to Corte, QQS, tango close. Figure ends facing diagonal wall.

14. Promenade Pivot begins in promenade position facing diagonal wall SSQQ Walk in promenade position then step across in front of partner with the right foot on the second S, then 3 pivots to right Figure ends promenade position, SS steps 1 & 2 of promenade turning left, QQQQS forward walk and side check tango close (steps 7-11 of running steps).

15. Oversway begins in promenade position facing diagonal wall, SQQS, in closed promenade, SSS Challenge line to Oversway & recover to fallaway position, QQS Whisk tap from fallaway position to promenade position.

Tango Bronze American Variations

1. Face to Face, Back-to-back (Waltz) begins in promenade position facing line of dance, SSQQS, open fan from promenade, QQS Twinkle from outside closed position to face to face, QQS twinkle from face to face to back-to-back, SS, pivot and crossover, QQS, tango close.

2. Progressive Twinkles (Waltz) begins in left outside position facing line of dance, QQS, twinkle open, QQS's Outside partner with turns on the at the end of each QQS, close up going right with SS, swivel point swivel point, QQS tango close

3. Grapevine (Waltz) begins in closed position facing diagonal wall, QQS, left foot diagonal forward left side lead, right foot forward in CBMP right outside partner, turning 1/4 R, left foot closes to right foot left outside position, QQS, back tango close, right foot back in left outside position, left foot side in left outside position, right foot close closed position.

4. Fallaway and Rock (Waltz) begins in facing diagonal center in closed position Figure ends facing diagonal center,
Measure 1 QQS twinkle from closed position to Fallaway position which is promenade position backing line of dance,
Measure 2 QQS Fallaway in promenade position, back 1, back 2, slip pivot on 3 (step back off the track closed position) left foot stays forward in CBMP,
Measure 3 QQS three left turning rock steps in CBMP
Measure 4 QQS back tango close closed position, ending facing wall. Note all the rotation is lead from the bottom.

5. Promenade Underarm Turn (Foxtrot) begins in promenade position facing W moving line of dance, SSQQQQ, left foot forward line of dance in CBMP, right foot forward line of dance in CBMP, turn right to face partner left foot side, right foot closes to left foot, left foot side, right foot closes to left foot. Figure ends facing wall. Partner's outside under arm turn is a spiral turn lead on the second slow completed on QQ. Lady does step side together on second QQ.

6. Zig Zag Outside Partner (Foxtrot) begins in closed position facing diagonal wall, SSQQ, 2 forward walks closed position to right outside partner, Chasse turning RP preparing to go left outside position, SSQQ, 2 back walks left outside position, Chasse turning left closed position. QQS tango close turning left. Figure ends facing diagonal center.

7. Fallaway Twinkles (Foxtrot) begins in closed position facing wall, each Measure SQQ,
Measure 1 twinkle from closed position to promenade position,
Measure 2 twinkle from promenade position to Fallaway position promenade position (forward, forward, close),

Measure 3 twinkle from Fallaway position promenade position to promenade position (back, back, close),

Measure 4 Twinkle close (facing S close). Figure ends closed position facing wall.

8. Promenade Twist (Foxtrot) Twist begins in promenade position facing wall moving line of dance, SS 2 walks in promenade position turning left 1/8, QQ twist to 3/8 turn left from promenade position to closed position on the ball of right foot and foot pressure on the B of the LR, QQ rock turn to left (left foot then right foot), SS forward walks turning L, QQS tango close. Figure ends closed position facing line of dance.

9. Fifth Position Breaks (V. Waltz) begins in closed position facing W, 5th position break to left (left foot side, right foot behind left foot, replace weight on left foot), 5th position break to the right, now that you are in promenade position facing line of dance, end with promenade turning left SSQQS. Figure ends closed position facing line of dance.

10. Left Rock Turn (Foxtrot) begins in closed position facing line of dance (can be used in any alinement to make a 1/8 to 3/8 turn to the left), SS, left foot forward right foot brushes toward left foot, right foot back and off the track left foot brushes to right foot beg turn L, QQS, tango close, (left foot forward completing left turn, right foot side, left foot brushes to right foot), Figure ends facing C. Add under arm turn on the back side together.

Tango American Silver Figures

1. Quick Right Turn begins in promenade position facing diagonal wall, SQQQ, walk in promenade position and three steps of a passing right turn (left foot side, right foot forward in CBMP, 3/8 right turn, left foot side and slightly back to closed position, right foot back right side leading prep right outside partner), QS, turn from right outside partner to promenade position (left foot back in CBMP right outside partner, ¼ right turn, right foot side left foot held side w/o weight), SQQQ, walk in promenade position and twist turn to promenade position Figure ends in closed position (1/8 left turn, left foot side, 1/8 left turn, right foot forward and across in CBMP, 1/8 left turn, twist to left allowing feet to uncross, 1/4 left turn, end weight on right foot, foot almost closed), QQQ, tango close.

2. Oversway & Rondé promenade position begins in facing line of dance, SS two steps of Promenade Left turn, QQ&, forward ½ of a reverse turn from Viennese Waltz, QQS, Back walk to Challenge Line and Oversway, S, Right lunge leading Rondé, QQQQ, lead Fallaway Pivot to left and closed finish.

3. Fallaway Fan begins in promenade position facing diagonal wall, SQQS, Closed Promenade (International figure) with Rondé, QQSS, and lead Fallaway grapevine to outside swivel and left promenade pivot, QQS, tango close.

4. Cobra Fans begins in promenade position facing diagonal wall, SSQQ, promenade walk to right pivots, SSSS, in-line swivel, promenade pivot, QQ, part of tango close.

5. Fallaway Rondé begins in promenade position facing diagonal wall, SQQS three steps of Quick Right Turn and Fallaway Rondé, QQSS, (1-2 forward, 3 forward, 4 turn right to cut off partner, 5 steps back, 6* ronde left foot *really on 5, 7, 8 slip pivot with 90 turn left E DW closed). The figure can be considered complete here or continued with a Fallaway grapevine to outside swivel and left promenade, to tango close.

6. Spanish Drag begins in closed position facing diagonal wall, SSQQ, two forward walks to back rock, SSSS, left lunge and draw left foot in Spanish Drag Position, &S, Close and tap in promenade position.

7. Change of Place begins in promenade position facing diagonal wall, SSQ&QS, three promenade walks leading under arm turn left, in in left side partner, QQS, free spin left in left side partner to right side partner (change of places), QQS, spin right, right side partner to left side partner (change of places), SSQQS, open fan from left side partner to closed position, tango close.

8. Outside Underarm Turn to Shadow Position begins in closed position facing diagonal wall, QQ, two steps of reverse turn, preparing to lead Follower for an under arm turn right, QQQ, back, side, close (followers under arm turn right), QS, right foot side, receiving follower in right Shadow Position.

9. Shadow Drag begins in right Shadow Position facing diagonal wall, SSS&S, two steps in left outside position, shadow drag and recover, QQS, left foot side rock (follower's free spin left) end in left side partner, SS, open fan from left side partner to closed position.

10. Swivel Fans begins in promenade position facing diagonal wall, SSQQ, 1-3 of Quick Right Turn, right foot side preparing for Swivel Fans in Double hand hold, SSSQQ, 4 side rocks and quick Swivel Fans), left foot side in prep for left outside position, S, back check in left outside position, QQSQQS, reverse turn from left outside position (starting in double hand hold)

11. Pivots to Fallaway Whisk begins in promenade position facing diagonal wall, SSQQQ, walk in promenade position to promenade pivot, 2 pivots to right, QS FR back to Fallaway Whisk, SQQS, Lead left promenade pivot, tango close.

12. Shadow Rocks begins in right Shadow Position facing line of dance, SS, 2 walks in right shadow position, QQS, left foot forward rock in right shadow position, QQS, left foot side rock (follower's free spin L) end in left side partner, SQQS, open fan and tango close for left side partner to closed position.

13. Reverse Outside Swivel begins in closed position facing diagonal center, QQS, 2 steps of reverse turn, swivel to promenade position, QQQQ, lead left promenade pivot to tango close.

14. Traveling Right Lunges begins in promenade position facing diagonal wall, SS, 2 walks in promenade position, swivel to right lunge position on 2nd walk, SS 2 walks in promenade position swivel to right lunge position on 2nd walk, SSQQS Promenade left turn.

15. Same Foot Lunge with Rock Ending begins in promenade position facing diagonal wall, QQ, promenade chassé, SQQ, first three steps of Quick Right Turn, QQ, right chasse leading follower to same foot lung position. SQQ, Same foot lunge and swivel to forward left pivot, QQS, 2nd half of Reverse Turn (Closed Finish).

16. Footwork into the Corner (not syllabus) 1 forward 2&3 to the side look into corner, 4 look promenade, 5 hold, 6 hook, & replace, 7 point P, 8 hold F NLOD DC PP.

17. Promenade to Closed (not a syllabus figure) starts in PP with two walks SS then forward Q close right foot to left changing weight Q then bring partner to the left into closed position on the &.

18. Viennese Cross (not syllabus) 1 left foot forward turning left, right foot side turning left, & left crosses in front of the right foot (the Cross) turning left, right foot back in "Ugly Foot" position turning left, left foot side turning left.

Tango – International Bronze Figures

1. Progressive Link begins in closed position facing diagonal wall, QQ, left foot forward in CBMP right side lead, right foot side and slightly back in promenade position. Figure ends promenade position facing diagonal wall.

2. Closed Promenade begins in promenade position along line of dance, SQQS, left foot side, right foot forward and across in CBMP, left foot to side and slightly forward, right foot closes to left foot slightly back.

3. Progressive Side Step begins QQS, left foot forward in CBMP, right foot to side and slightly back, left foot forward in CBMP.

4. Progressive Side Step Reverse Turn begins in closed position facing diagonal center, QQSS, left foot forward in CBMP, ¾ turn to left (for the whole figure?), right foot side and slightly back, left foot forward in CBMP, right foot forward right side lead, QQS, transfer weight back to left foot left side lead, transfer weight back to right foot, left foot back small step left side lead, QQS, right foot back in CBMP, left foot to side and slightly back, right foot closes to left foot slightly back. Figure ends closed position facing diagonal wall. After first four steps, a back Corté SQQS or a rock on the SF, rock on the right foot, back Corte QQS QQS SQQS can be substituted for the reverse turn.

5. Natural Twist Turn begins in promenade position pointing diagonal wall along line of dance, SQQ, left foot to side in promenade position, right foot forward and across on promenade position and CBMP, left foot to side, SQQ, right foot crosses behind left foot, commence twist to right allowing feet to uncross, feet almost closed weight on right foot in promenade position facing diagonal wall. Amounts of turn may vary.

6. Natural Rock Turn begins in closed position facing diagonal wall, SQQ. right foot forward, left foot to side and slightly back, transfer weight ford to right foot right side leading, ¼ turn right over these three steps, SQQS, left foot back small step left side leading, right foot back in CBMP, left foot to side and slightly back, ¼ turn left over these three steps, right foot closes to left foot slightly back. Figure ends facing diagonal wall.

7. Natural Promenade Turn begins in promenade position facing diagonal wall along line of dance, SQQS, left foot to side in promenade position, right foot forward in promenade position and CBMP, left foot to side and slight back pivoting 180 R, right foot forward in CBMP pivoting 90 right left foot placed to side of right foot w/o weight.

8. Open Promenade begins in promenade position facing diagonal wall along line of dance, SQQS, left foot to side in promenade position, right foot forward and across in CBMP, left foot to side and slightly forward, right foot forward in CBMP outside partner. Figure ends outside partner facing between wall and diagonal wall.

9. Open Reverse Turn Partner Outside begins in closed position facing diagonal center, QQS, left foot forward in CBMP, right foot to side, left foot back in CBMP, QQS, right foot back, left foot to side and slightly forward, right foot closes to left foot slightly back. Figure ends closed position facing diagonal wall. ¾ turn to right made over the entire figure.

10. Back Corté begins in closed position along line of dance, SQQS, left foot back left side leading, right foot back in CBMP, left foot to side and slight forward, FR closes to left foot slightly back. ¼ turn left between 2 and 3. Figure ends closed position facing diagonal wall.

11. Left foot Rock begins in closed position along line of dance, QQS, left foot back left side leading, transfer weight forward to right foot right side leading, left foot back small step left side leading.

12. Right Foot Rock begins in closed position along line of dance, right foot back in CBMP, transfer weight forward to left foot in CBMP, right foot back small step in CBMP.

13. Basic Reverse Turn begins in closed position facing diagonal center, QQS, left foot forward in CBMP, right foot to side and slightly back, left foot crosses in front of right foot, QQS, right foot back, left foot to side and slightly forward, right foot closes to left foot slightly back. ¾ turn to the left over the entire figure. Figure ends closed position facing diagonal wall.

14. Open Reverse Turn in Line begins in closed position facing diagonal center. QQS, left foot forward in CBMP, right foot to side and slightly back, left foot back left side leading, QQS, right foot back in CBMP, left foot to side and slightly forward, right foot closes to left foot slightly back. ¾ turn to the left over the entire figure. Figure ends closed position facing diagonal wall

Tango - International Silver

16) Four Step begins in facing wall, QQQQ, left foot forward, 1/8 turn to left, right foot side and slightly back, left foot back in CBMP, right foot closes to left foot slightly back in promenade position. Figure ends diagonal wall.

17) Promenade Link begins in promenade position along line of dance, SQQ, left foot forward in promenade position, right foot forward in promenade position with 1/8 turn to right, left foot side without weight while bringing partner to closed position.

18A) Outside Swivel begins in diagonal center, QQSQQ, left foot forward beginning ½ turn to left over the first three steps, right foot side, left foot back in CBMP right foot moves left in front of left foot without weight in promenade position, turn 1/8 left, right foot forward and across in promenade position, left foot place to side of right foot without weight while partner rotates to closed position.

18B) Outside Swivel, Taken from Open Promenade Commences after open promenade (bronze figure 8) which ends outside partner, diagonal center Aline of dance, SQQ, left foot back in CBMP right foot crosses in front of left foot without weight into promenade position, right foot forward and across in promenade position, left foot paced to side of right foot without weight. Figure ends diagonal wall. One swivel and rotate partner to closed position.

18C) Outside Swivel, Taken from Open Promenade, Turning Left Commences after open promenade (bronze figure 8) which ends OP, Aline of dance, SQQ, left foot back in CBMP right foot crosses in front of left foot without weight into promenade position, right foot forward and across in promenade position, left foot paced to side of right foot without weight. Figure ends diagonal center. One swivel and rotate partner to closed position.

19) Fallaway Promenade begins in promenade position, line of dance, SQQ promenade moving forward curving to the right, SQQ promenade moving backward. Figure ends W.

20) Brush Tap begins in closed position, diagonal wall, QQ&S, left foot forward, turn left 1/8, right foot side, left foot brushes to right foot no weight, left foot place to the side right foot no weight. Figure ends line of dance.

21) Four Step Change begins in closed position, diagonal wall, QQ&S, left foot forward, right foot side and slightly back, left foot closes to right foot, right foot back small step. Figure ends diagonal wall Aline of dance.

22) Back Open Promenade begins in promenade position, line of dance, SQQS, left foot side, right foot forward and across in promenade position, ¼ to 3/8 turn right, left foot side and slightly back to closed position, right foot back closed position. Figure ends backing diagonal center.

Foxtrot

Key characteristics of the Foxtrot are smooth, gliding steps with a heel lead, controlled movement and an easygoing look. The Foxtrot is an all-purpose dance that can be performed to many different styles of music. At the Silver level, the style changes to continuity movement which means the feet continue to pass each other rather than close as in the Bronze Foxtrot. These passing steps are long, smooth, continuous, and flowing.

Rise and fall are similar to Waltz, but less pronounced than in Waltz because emphasis in Foxtrot is on progression. Rise and fall should be smooth and gradual.

Foxtrot Bronze American Figures

1. Basic begins in closed position facing line of dance.
In bronze basic rhythm, SSQQ, move left foot forward, right foot forward, left foot side and slightly forward, right foot closes to left foot.
In box rhythm, SQQ, move left foot forward, right foot side and slightly forward, left foot closes to right foot.
2. Promenade begins in closed position facing wall, SSQQ, turn to promenade position left foot forward line of dance in CBMP, right foot forward line of dance in CBMP, turn right to face partner left foot side facing wall, right foot closes to left foot end facing wall.
3A. Rock Turn to Left (Left Rock Turn) starts forward and turn on the back rock. closed position facing line of dance (can be used in any alinement to make a 1/8 to 3/8 turn to the left), SSQQ, left foot forward right foot brushes toward left foot, right foot back and off the track left foot brushes to right foot beg turn left, left foot side completing left turn, right foot closes to left foot, Figure ends facing center. Add under arm turn on the back side together.
3B. Rock Turn to Right (Right Rock Turn) Starts backward and turn on the forward rock. closed position facing line of dance (can be used in any alinement to make a 1/8 to 3/8 turn to the right), SSQQ, left foot back right foot brushes toward left foot, right foot forward and left foot brushes to right foot beg turn R, left foot side completing right turn, right foot closes to left foot, Figure ends facing wall.
4. Sway Step begins in closed position facing W, SSQQ, left foot side right foot brushes to left foot, right foot Side left foot brushes to right foot, left foot side, right foot closes to left foot. Or step tap, step tap, step together, all quicks.
5A. Promenade Underarm Turn begins in closed position facing W, SSQQ, turn to promenade position left foot forward line of dance in CBMP, right foot forward line of dance in CBMP, turn right to face partner left foot side facing W,

right foot closes to left foot Figure ends facing wall. The outside under arm turn is on the SS

5B. Sway Underarm Turn SSQQ, begins step tap, step tap, step together. Outside under arm turn is on the step together.

6A. Zig Zag in Line SSQQ, begins in with two forward walks in closed position, Chasse turning R, SSQQ, two back walks closed position, Chasse turning L. Figure ends facing diagonal wall.

6B. Zig Zag Outside Partner SSQQ, begins with two forward walks closed position to right outside partner, Chasse turning preparing to go left outside position, SSQQ, 2 back walks left outside position, Chasse turning left closed position. Figure ends facing diagonal wall.

7. Box Step SQQ, **Forward ½ Box,** begins in left foot forward, right foot side, left foot closes to right foot, SQQ, **Back ½ of Box**, right foot back, left foot side, right foot closes to left foot. Use any alignment with 0 to 3/8 turn.

8. Twinkle (box rhythm, SQQ) begins in closed position facing wall,

Twinkle Open, from closed position to promenade position, left foot forward, right foot side and slightly forward, turning 1/8 to L, left foot closes to right in promenade position.

Twinkle Close, from promenade position to closed position, right foot forward and across in CBMP commencing to turn right closed position, left foot side completing 1/8 turn to R, right foot closes to left foot. Figure ends facing wall.

9. Promenade Twinkles begins in closed position facing wall all Measure SQQ, Measure 1 twinkle from closed position to overturned promenade position(OT promenade position), Measure 2 twinkle from promenade position to left side partner, Measure 3 twinkle from open counter promenade (O closed position) to OT promenade position, Measure 4 twinkle close from promenade position to closed position. Roll out turn or closed turn, turn back, twinkle close

10. Fallaway Twinkles are twinkles to promenade position, forward and back in promenade position, close. Ends in closed position facing wall, each measure is SQQ,

Measure 1 is a twinkle from closed position to promenade position,

Measure 2 is a twinkle from promenade position to Fallaway position promenade position (forward. forward. close),

Measure 3 is a twinkle from Fallaway position promenade position to promenade position (back, back, close),

Measure 4 is a twinkle close (forward side close). Figure ends closed position facing wall.

11. Turning Twinkles to Outside Partner begins in closed position facing wall

Measure 1 SQQ is a twinkle open,

Measure 2 SQQ is a twinkle from promenade position to prep right outside partner (right outside position),

Measure 3 S<u>S</u>QQ is a rock turn to right from right outside partner to closed position

12. Grapevine begins facing diagonal wall SSQQ S <u>6</u>Q (up on Q's 1 3 5) SQQ, forward ½ of Zig Zag in line, left foot back then six grapevine steps(R back, left side, right forward, left side, right back left side) alternating left outside partner and right outside partner, steps 2-4 of Zig Zag OP. Figure ends closed position facing wall.

13. Promenade Twist begins in closed position facing line of dance, SS 2 walks in promenade position turning left 1/8, QQ twist to 3/8 turn left from promenade position to closed position on the ball of right foot and foot pressure on the B of the LR, SSQQ rock turn to left. Figure ends facing W.

14. Promenade Pivot begins in closed position facing W, SSQQ, left foot side promenade position, 1/8 right turn, right foot forward in CBMP with pivoting action and 3/8 right turn promenade position to closed position, left foot side and slightly back off the track ugly foot with ½ right turn closed position, right foot forward prep promenade position, 1/8 turn R, SSQQ, left foot forward promenade position, FR forward and across in CBMP, 1/8 right turn, left foot side closed position, right foot closes to left foot. Figure ends facing W.

15A. Running Steps in Basic Rhythm begins in facing line of dance SSQQ (QQ outside partner, passing feet with rise) SSQQ basic in line.

15B. Running Steps in Box Rhythm begins in facing line of dance SQQ passing feet with rise SQQ basic all steps in line.

Foxtrot Bronze American Variations

1. Single Corté (Tango) begins in closed position facing line of dance, SSQQ 1 forward basic, SSQQ step back with left foot leaving right foot forward, replace weight to right foot, left foot side with ¼ turn R, close right foot to left foot changing weight, Figure ends facing wall in closed position.

2. Twist Turn to Right (Tango) begins in promenade position facing wall along line of dance, SSQQ, left foot forward, right foot forward and across in CBMP, ¼ turn R, left foot side closed position,1/8 turn R, right foot crosses behind left foot prep right outside partner, SSQQ, start to twist right allowing feet to uncross in right outside partner, Weight on right foot left foot side without weight, left foot side, right foot close to left foot. Figure ends facing diagonal wall of new line of dance.

3A. Fifth Position Breaks (V. Waltz) begins in closed position facing line of dance, SQQ 5th position break to left (left foot side, right foot behind left foot, replace weight on left foot), SQQ 5th position break to the R, SQQ end with forward ½ box turning to face diagonal center or SSQQ basic facing line of dance.

3B. Fifth Position Breaks with Underarm Turn (V. Waltz) begins in closed position facing line of dance, SQQ 5th position break to left (left foot side, right foot behind left foot, replace weight on left foot), SQQ 5th position break to the right opening to lead turn, SQQ 5th position break to the left leading outside under arm turn, SQQ end with forward ½ box turning to face diagonal center or SSQQ basic facing line of dance.

4A. Cross Body Lead (V. Waltz) begins in closed position facing along the line of dance, SSQQ, left foot forward right foot brushing to left foot, right foot back and off the track, right foot side leading partner across, left foot Closes to right foot making a 180 turn with the 4 steps, SQQ forward ½ box or SSQQ basic to finish. Figure ends facing line of dance.

4B. Cross Body Lead with Underarm Turn (V. Waltz) begins in closed position facing line of dance, SSQQ left foot forward right foot brushing to left foot, right foot back and off the track leading an inside under arm turn for partner, right foot side leading partner across, left foot Closes to right foot making a 180 turn with the 4 steps, SQQ forward ½ box or SSQQ basic to finish. Figure ends facing line of dance.

5. Two Way Underarm Turn (Waltz) begins facing line of dance and ends facing wall,

Measure 1 SQQ for ½ of box,

Measure 2 SQQ back ½ of box leading partner to an under-arm turn (under arm turn) off to the left side,

Measure 3 SQQ twinkle forward from outside closed position to offset right partner & lead partner to step forward and side into opposing stretch positions,

Measure 4 SQQ twinkle from Offset RP to left side partner lead under arm turn (forward, side, together and turn),

Measure 5 SQQ twinkle from outside closed position to promenade position collecting partner,

Measure 6 SQQ is a twinkle close from promenade position to closed position.

Figure can be used without the first two Measures to end face to face, back-to-back facing BB

6. Face to Face, Back-to-back (Waltz) begins facing line of dance and ends facing center.

Measure 1 SQQ forward half of box,

Measure 2 SQQ back half of box with a under arm turn,

Measure 3 SQQ Twinkle from outside closed position to face to face, Measure 4 SQQ twinkle from face to facing to back-to-back,

Measure 5 SQQ twinkle from BB to promenade position,

Measure 6 SQQ Twinkle from promenade position to closed position (twinkle close).

An under arm turn or Spin turn can be added on the forward movements. A two way under arm turn can be used as an alternate ending.

7. Progressive Twinkles (Waltz) begins facing line of dance outside partner with turns on the end of each Measure, close up going right.

Measure 1 SQQ is a twinkle from closed position to right outside partner, Measure 2 SQQ is a twinkle from right outside partner to left outside position,

Measure 3 SQQ is a twinkle from left outside position to right outside partner,

Measure 4 SQQ is a twinkle from right outside partner to closed position. This figure can also be done in two hand hold.

8. Promenade Chassé (Waltz) begins facing diagonal wall, SQQ twinkle open, forward SQ&Q in promenade position, SQQ twinkle ending.

8A. Chasse' to the side is also used when leading partner for a spin or an under-arm turn.

9. Fallaway and Basic (Waltz) begins facing diagonal center in closed position and ends facing diagonal center,

Measure 1 SQQ twinkle from closed position to Fallaway position which is promenade position backing line of dance,

Measure 2 SQQ Fallaway in promenade position back 1 back 2, slip pivot on 3 (step back off the track closed position),

Measure 3 SQQ forward half of under turned left turning box in closed position,

Measure 4 SQQ back half of under turned left turning box in closed position, Figure ends diagonal center

Measures 3-4 can be replaced with SSQQ basic ending closed position W.

10. Twinkle & Weave (Waltz) begins facing diagonal wall in closed position and ends facing line of dance closed position

Measure 1 SQQ Twinkle for closed position to promenade position,

Measure 2 SQQ Weave from promenade position turning <u>left</u> on 2nd step to right outside partner 3rd step back & side,

Measure 3 SQQ Back twinkle turning <u>right</u> from right outside partner to promenade position,

Measure 4 SQQ Twinkle close from promenade position to closed position, Figure ends diagonal wall

11. Check & Developé (Waltz) begins in open left outside position in double hand hold facing diagonal center.

Measure 1 move the left foot forward and across in CBMP for a check in left outside open partner position while raising hands to lead follower's Developé, which is to lean back while raising the left leg almost to leader's armpit. The position is held for 2 3. The checking foot can be turned out for stability.

Measure 2 move right foot back in CBMP, move left foot to the side rotating the top to the left 180 and brushing the right foot to the left, then right foot back.

Clarke Fairbrother – Dance Nuggets

Measure 3 move the left foot back in CBMP, move the right foot to the left foot making a heal turn, an open impetus, collecting partner from two hand hold into promenade position and a forward step with the left in promenade position. Figure ends facing diagonal center.
An alternative measure 3 would be to lead a spin turn from the open position.

To add Rumba or Mambo figures as alternatives for Foxtrot or Waltz, add an extra side step to a box step and then use open break or checking figures. Examples are:
Open break with alternating under arm turns (Rumba)
Cross body lead with inside underarm turn (Rumba)
Peek a Boo (Shoulder Check) from open break (Rumba)
Cradle Circle (Rumba)
Cross over break to Ieta (Rumba)
Sliding Doors (Rumba)
Mambo crossing swivels
Slow underarm turn (Rumba & Waltz)
Natural or Reverse tops
5th position, cross body lead, change of places (V Waltz)

Foxtrot Silver American Figures

Many figures are shown starting closed position with a twinkle to promenade position and end with a twinkle close to closed position. These starting and ending twinkles can be omitted if already in promenade position or staying in promenade position.

1. Open Left Box begins in closed position facing diagonal center, SQQ, first half of Open Left Box, left foot forward, ¼ left turn, right foot side prep right outside partner, 1/8 turn L, left foot back in CBMP right outside partner, SQQ, second half of Open Left Box, right foot forward closed position, 3/8 left turn, left foot side and slightly forward prep right outside partner, right foot forward in CBMP right outside partner. Figure ends facing diagonal wall.

2. Open Right Turn begins in closed position facing diagonal wall, SQQ, twinkle from closed position to promenade position, SQQ Leader's passing right 3/8 turn from promenade position to right outside partner, SQQ Heel turn right 3/8 from right outside partner to promenade position(open impetus), SQQ continuity ending promenade position to right outside partner. Figure ends facing diagonal center.

3. Grapevine begins in closed position facing diagonal wall, SQQ twinkle from closed position to promenade position, SQQ Leader's passing right turn from promenade position to right outside partner, QQQQ left foot back grapevine from right outside partner, SQQ Heal turn right outside partner to promenade position, Figure ends facing line of dance diagonal center

4. Weave from Promenade begins in promenade position diagonal center, SQQ, right foot forward in CBMP, left foot forward between partner's feet, ¼ turn L, right foot side and slightly back prep right outside partner, 1/8 turn L, QQQQ, left foot back in CBMP right outside partner, right foot back closed position, 3/8 turn L, left foot side and slightly forward prep right outside partner, right foot forward in CBMP right outside partner. Figure ends facing diagonal wall.

5. Chair & Slip begins in closed position facing diagonal wall, SQQ, twinkle to promenade position, SQQ, Chair (promenade check two steps) right foot forward and across in CBMP, replace weight to left foot in CBMP, Slip Pivot (one back step on right foot pivoting L) right foot back small step pivot left foot held in CBMP with ¼ turn L. D facing diagonal center. Amount of turn on the Slip Pivot can vary.

6. Oversway begins in closed position facing diagonal center, SQQ, first half of Open Left Box end right outside partner, SQQS, closed position back into Challenge Line and Oversway, QQ Recovery to promenade position, FR closes to left foot, left foot side, figure ends facing diagonal wall.

7A. Hairpin from Reverse (Open left Box) begins in closed position facing diagonal center, SQQ, first half of Open Left Box, SQQ, starts closed position right foot back check and forward curving run to right outside partner (Hairpin), SQQ heel turn from right outside partner to promenade position (Impetus). Figure ends facing line of dance

7B. Hairpin from Promenade Position begins in closed position facing diagonal wall, SQQ, twinkle to promenade position, SQQ, walk in promenade position forward curving to the right, to right outside partner (Hairpin), SQQ, Heel turn from right outside partner to promenade position (Impetus). Figure ends facing line of dance.

8. Slide & Check begins in closed position facing diagonal wall, SS, left foot forward, right foot diagonally forward right side leading left foot closes to right foot slightly forward no weight ¼ turn L, SSS, contra check and back turning hover to promenade position, 1/8 turn L, left foot forward in CBMP, 1/8 left turn, replace weight to right foot 1/4 right turn prep promenade position, left foot side ¼ turn L. Figure ends facing line of dance.

9. Fallaway & Weave begins in closed position facing diagonal center, S&QQ, Syncopated Fallaway to right outside partner Bounce Fallaway, left foot forward, ¼ turn L, right foot side and slightly back in Fallaway position, 1/8 turn L, left foot back and across in CBMP, right foot side and slightly back prep right outside partner, QQQQ, weave ending, left foot back in CBMP right outside partner, right foot back closed position, Left foot side and slightly forward prep right outside partner, right foot forward in CBMP right outside partner. Figure ends facing diagonal wall.

10. Curved Running Steps begins in closed position facing diagonal center, SQQ, left foot forward running steps curving L, SQQ, right foot back running steps curving L, SQQ, left foot forward running steps curving L, SQQ, back half of Open Left Box to right outside partner. Figure ends facing diagonal wall.

11. Natural Fallaway begins in closed position facing diagonal wall, SQQ, twinkle to promenade position, SQQ, Leader's passing right turn from promenade position to Fallaway position, SQQ, Heel turn from Fallaway position to promenade position. Figure ends facing line of dance.

12. Outside Swivel begins in closed position facing diagonal wall, SQQ, twinkle to promenade position, SQQ Leader's passing right to from promenade position to right outside partner, SQQ, left foot back (follower's outside swivel) the Lilt (aka Cantors, rise and fall over two steps instead of three) (Follower's promenade pivot) pivot, SQQ Under turned second half of Open Left Box. Figure ends facing diagonal wall.

13. Hover Corté begins in closed position facing diagonal center, SQQ, first half of Open Left Box, SQQ, right foot back to Hover Corte (right foot back, 3/8 left turn, left foot side and slightly forward, replace weight to right foot side and slightly back prep right outside partner), SQQ, left foot back twinkle from right outside partner to promenade position (left foot back in CBMP, right foot back prep promenade position, ¼ left turn, left foot side. Figure ends facing line of dance.

14. Promenade Pivot begins in closed position facing diagonal wall, SQQ, twinkle to promenade position, SQQ Right promenade pivots, SQQ, Heel turn from closed position to promenade position, Figure ends facing line of dance

15. The Gem begins in closed position facing diagonal center, SQQ, first half of Open Left Box, SQQ, 3 back steps from closed position to left outside partner, SQQ, left foot forward swivel from left outside position to right outside partner hover to promenade position. Figure ends facing diagonal wall.

16. Tossing Grapevine (not syllabus) in shadow position behind partner, 8Qs, 1 right foot crossing in front of left forward down the LOD while facing W, in CBMP, then 2 rotate bottom the other direction to be backing LOD maintaining top parallel to wall and step back with left. 3 Step back with the right rotate bottom and 4 step side with the left, tossing partner to your left hand as she gets ahead of you in the movement. Repeat 1 &2 tossing partner back to your right hand as you get ahead of her in the movement. Repeat 3&4. End with SQ&Q chasse with spin for partner.

Foxtrot Bronze International

1. Feather Step begins in closed position facing line of dance diagonal center or diagonal wall, SQQ, **starts with right side lead, right foot** forward, left foot forward prep to go OSP, right foot forward OP, ends with left side lead, footwork is heel toe, toe, toe heel (HT T TH).

2. Reverse Turn with Feather Finish begins in closed position facing diagonal center, SQQ, left foot forward, turn ¼ L, right foot side turning 1/8 left, left foot back, SQQ, right foot back beginning to turn, 3/8 turn, left foot to side and slightly forward, right foot forward in CBMP, Figure ends facing diagonal wall, ends with left side lead.

3. Three Step begins in closed position facing line of dance or diagonal wall, SQQ, **starts with left side lead, left foot forward**, right foot forward (HT), left foot forward, Figure ends facing line of dance, ends with right side lead, footwork HT HT TH.

4. Natural Turn begins in closed position facing line of dance, SQQSSS, right foot forward beginning to turn R, 3/8 right turn, left foot side, 1/8 turn, right foot back, left foot back beginning to turn R, 3/8 turn, right foot to side small step heel pull, left foot forward, Figure ends facing diagonal center. Amounts of turn and directions may vary. HT T TH TH H rolling to IE of left foot H.

5. Basic Weave begins in closed position facing diagonal center Aline of dance, QQQQQQ, left foot forward, 1/8 left turn, right foot side, 1/8 left turn, left foot back in CBMP, right foot back, ¼ turn left, left foot to side and slightly forward, RR forward in CBMP OP Figure ends facing diagonal wall. HT T T T T TH.

6. Reverse Wave begins in closed position facing line of dance, SQQ SQQ SSS, left foot forward, ¼ left turn, right foot side, 1/8 turn L, left foot back, right foot back, 1/8 turn L, right foot back, left foot back, 3/8 left turn, right foot to side small step heel pull, left foot forward, Figure ends facing diagonal center. HT T TH TH T TH TH H then IE of left foot H.

7. Change of Direction begins in closed position facing diagonal wall, SSS, left foot forward, ¼ left turn, right foot diagonal back left side lead and close to right foot to left foot slightly back w/o weight, left foot forward in CBMP. Figure ends facing diagonal center.

8. Natural Weave begins in closed position facing line of dance, SQQQQQQ, right foot forward, 3/8 right turn, left foot side, slight right turn, right foot back right-side lead, right foot back, ¼ left turn, left foot to side and slightly forward, right foot forward in DBMP OP. Figure ends facing diagonal wall. HT T T T T T TH.

9. Closed Impetus with Feather Finish begins in closed position beginning line of dance, SQQ SQQ, left foot back, 3/8 right turn, right foot closes to left foot (heel turn), ¼ right turn, left foot to side and slightly back, right foot back, ¼ left turn, left foot side and slightly forward, right foot forward in CBMP OP. Figure ends facing diagonal center.

Foxtrot – International Silver

10. Quick Open Reverse begins in closed position, diagonal center, SQ&QQQ, left foot forward, ¼ turn left, right foot side, 1/8 turn left, Left foot back, right foot back, 3/8 turn left, left foot side and slightly back, right foot forward in CBMP OP. Figure ends diagonal wall.

11. Quick Natural Weave closed position, diagonal wall, SQ&Q SQQ right foot forward, ¼ turn right, left foot side, right foot back right side leading, left foot back, right foot back, ¼ turn left, left foot side and slightly forward, right foot forward in CBMP OP. Figure ends diagonal wall

12. Top Spin (After Feather Finish) begins at a corner backing line of dance, QQQQ, left foot back 1/8 turn left, right foot back 1/8 turn left, left foot side and slightly forward ¼ turn left, right foot forward OP. Figure ends diagonal center new line of dance.

13. Hover Telemark begins diagonal wall, SQQ, left foot forward, 1/8 turn left, right foot side then left foot brushes right foot, left foot side and slightly forward.

Figure ends diagonal center promenade position. Step 1 of the following figure will be outside partner.

14A. Natural Twist Turn with Hover Feather Ending begins in line of dance, **Twist turn:** SQ&QS, right foot forward, 3/8 turn right, left foot side, 1/8 turn right, right foot crosses behind left foot slightly back, twist on both feet end with right foot to side small step (on QS), **Hover Feather Ending:** QQ, left foot diagonal forward preparing to step OP left side leading, right foot forward in CBMP OP. Figure ends diagonal center.

14B. Natural Twist Turn with Closed Impetus & Feather Finish Ending Twist turn, Impetus: Q, left foot back and to the left, Feather finish: SQQ, back into feather finish.

14C. Natural Twist Turn with Open Impetus Ending Twist turn, Impetus ending: QS, left foot diagonal forward left side lead, right foot forward in promenade position pointing diagonal center facing line of dance.

14D. Natural Twist Turn with Natural Weave Ending twist turn ending with right foot forward and slightly side facing line of dance, Q, left foot side and slightly back backing diagonal center, natural weave: 5Q's.

15. Open Telemark, Natural Turn Outside Swivel with Feather Ending begins diagonal center, Open Telemark: SQQ, left foot forward, ¼ turn left, right foot side, ¼ left, left foot side in promenade position, Natural turn: SQQ, right foot forward and across in promenade position, 1/8 turn right, left foot side, 1/8 turn right, right foot back right side lead, Outside Swivel with feather ending: SSQQ, left foot back in CBMP and right foot crosses loosely in front without weight in promenade position(partner swivels), right foot forward and across in promenade position, left foot diagonal forward preparing to step OP left side leading, right foot forward in CBMP OP. Figure ends diagonal center.

16. Open Telemark with Feather Ending begins diagonal center, Open Telemark: SQQ, left foot forward, ¼ turn left, right foot side, ¼ left, left foot side in promenade position, Feather ending SQQ. Figure ends diagonal wall.

17. Open Impetus. Backing line of dance, SQQ, left foot back beg turn to R, 3/8 turn, right foot closes to left foot (heel turn), ¼ turn, left foot side and slightly back ending in promenade position.

The International syllabus uses the term "impetus" in Waltz, Foxtrot or Quickstep to describe **a heel turn for the man turning to the right**. The open impetus is one of several ways to get into promenade position and is used to turn dancers around corners or change their direction on the dance floor. It is often used after a natural turn. The open impetus has less turn for the man than the closed impetus. The closed impetus remains in closed position, while the open impetus ends in promenade position.

18. Weave from Promenade Position begins pointing diagonal center in promenade position, S 6Qs, right foot forward in promenade position, left foot forward, ¼ turn right, right foot side and slightly back, 1/8 turn right, right foot back, 3/8 turn right, left foot side and slightly forward, right foot forward in CBMP in promenade position. Figure ends diagonal wall.

19. Hover Cross begins diagonal wall, S 6Qs, right foot forward, ¼ right, left foot side small step, ½ turn right, left foot forward in CBMP outside partner on left side, transfer weight back to right foot in CBMP, ¼ turn left, left foot side and slightly forward, right foot forward in CBMP OP. Figure ends diagonal center.

20. Closed Telemark begins in closed position, diagonal center, SQQ, left foot forward beginning turn to left, right foot side turning 3/8 left, left foot side and slightly forward turning 3/8 left. Figure ends diagonal wall.

21. Natural Telemark begins diagonal wall, SQQQQ, right foot forward, ¼ turn right, left foot side, ½ turn right, right foot side small step, left foot diagonal preparing to step outside partner, left side leading, right foot forward in CBMP. Figure ends facing diagonal center

22. Hover Feather begins diagonal center, QQ, left foot diagonal forward preparing to step OP left side leading, right foot forward in DVMP OP. Figure ends diagonal center.

23. Reverse Pivot begins backing line of dance right foot back in CBMP small step turning up to ½ turn to left, left foot held in CBMP. This figure is just a S or a Q or an & count. This is like a slip pivot in some other dances.

Viennese Waltz

Viennese Waltz is characterized by its speed which is twice as fast as Waltz. Because of the speed, significantly less "rise and fall" and sway are used. At the Silver level, the style changes to Continuity Movement in some figures which means that the feet continue to pass each other rather than close as in the Bronze Viennese Waltz. These passing steps are smooth, continuous, and flowing.

Reverse turn starts facing diagonal wall, opposite of other dances. Natural turns start facing diagonal center.

All Measures 1 2 3 unless otherwise noted. Hesitation timing is 1, hold 2 3. Cantor timing is 1, hold 2, then 3, i.e. two steps per measure.

Viennese Waltz American Bronze Figures

1. Balance Steps: Forward, Back, Side to Side begins in closed position facing line of dance with Hesitation timing (H), left foot forward right foot closes to left foot, H, right foot back left foot closes to right foot, H, left foot side right foot closes to left foot, H, right foot side left foot closes to right foot. H is Hesitation timing is one movement to full measure.

2A. Fifth Position Breaks begins in closed position facing line of dance,
Measure 1 is left foot side, right foot behind left foot (5th position), replace weight to left foot,
Measure 2 is right foot side, left foot behind right foot (5th position) replace weight to right foot.

2B. Fifth Position Breaks with Underarm Turn begins in closed position facing line of dance,
Measure 1, left 5th position break,
Measure 2, right open break,
Measure 3 left 5th position break leading under arm turn right,
Measure 4 right 5th position break to closed position.

3. Reverse Turn begins in closed position facing diagonal wall,
Measure 1, 1/8 left turn, left foot forward, 1/4 turn, right foot side and slightly back, 1/8 turn, left foot crosses in front of right foot,
Measure 2, 1/8 left turn, right foot back and slightly side, 3/8 left turn, left foot side, right foot closes to left foot. Figure ends facing diagonal wall. Turn can be increased ¼ overall to navigate corners in the line of dance.

4. Closed Twinkle begins in closed position facing line of dance, twinkle open and twinkle close as in Bronze Waltz.

5A. Crossbody Lead begins in closed position facing diagonal wall,

Measure 1, forward half of reverse turn,

Measure 2 back half of reverse turn leading partner across. Figure ends closed position facing diagonal wall after making a full turn during the figure.

5B. Crossbody Lead with Underarm Turn begins in closed position facing diagonal wall, Measure 1 & 2 as in 5A above,

Measure 3, three forward runs (Follower under arm turn left),

Measure 4, right foot side Hesitation in left side partner,

Measure 5, left foot Hesitation in facing position,

Measure 6, right foot side Hesitation in left side partner,

Measure 7, twinkle from open closed position to promenade position, Measure 8, twinkle from closed position to promenade position (twinkle close).

6. Hand-to-hand begins left side partner facing line of dance, proceed with steps 1-12 of figure 5B, Measure 1, twinkle from left side partner to facing partner, twinkle from facing partner to Back-to-back Position, twinkle from back-to-back position to promenade position, Measure 4 twinkle close. Same figure as Face to Face, Back-to-back in Waltz. Keep low with minimum rise and fall.

7A. Forward Progressive Changes-

Left foot closed position facing line of dance, left foot forward, right foot diagonally forward right side leading, left foot closes to right foot. Like first half of a Waltz box.

Right Foot right foot forward, left foot diagonally forward left side leading, right foot closes to left foot. Like the second Measure of a Waltz progressive.

7B. Backward Progressive Changes-Right Foot begins in closed position facing line of dance,

Right foot back, left foot diagonally back left side leading, right foot closes to left foot. Like the second half of a Waltz box.

Left foot back, right foot diagonally back right-side lead, left foot closes to right foot.

8. Right Turn (Natural Turn) begins in closed position facing diagonal center, Measure 1, 1/8 right turn, right foot forward, 1/4 right turn, left foot side, 1/8 right turn, right foot closes to left foot,

Measure 2, 1/8 right turn, left foot back and slightly side, 3/8 right turn, right foot side, left foot closes to right foot. Figure ends facing diagonal center. Turn can be reduced ¼ overall to navigate corners in line of dance.

9. Change of Place commence in left side partner facing line of dance (precede with steps 1-12 of figure 5B),

Measure 1, Canter rhythm free spin from left side partner (changing places),

Measure 2, left foot side hesitation in RSP,

Measure 3, Canter rhythm free spin from RSP (changing places),

Measure 4, right foot side hesitation in left side partner, follow with figure 6 (hand-to-hand) or just the last two Measures of figure 6.

10. Curtsey & Bow commences in right side partner, facing line of dance, weight on right foot,
Measure 1 is preparation for bow from right side partner to open facing partner.
Measure 2 is Bow (follower's curtsey).
Measure 3 is a right foot forward balance step to closed position. Bow and Curtsey can be followed with side balances or 5th positions for variety.

Viennese Waltz American Silver
1. X Line begins closed position facing diagonal wall,
Measure 1, forward half of reverse turn,
Measure 2, back half of reverse turn,
Measure 3, left foot forward to commence lead to Left X Line,
Measure 4, complete Left X Line and recover,
Measure 5 forward half of natural turn,
Measure 6 back half of natural turn,
Measure 7 left foot forward to commence to lead Right X Line,
Measure 8 complete Right X Line and recover.
2. Flairs Forward & Back begins closed position facing diagonal wall,
Measure 1, left foot forward swivel and point (flair) from closed position to right outside partner,
Measure 2, right foot forward swivel and point (Flair) from right outside partner to left outside partner position,
Measure 3, forward half of reverse turn from left outside partner position,
Measure 4, FR back swivel and point (Flair) from closed position to right outside partner,
Measure 5 left foot back swivel and point (Flair) from right outside partner to left outside position
Measure 6 is the back half of reverse turn from left outside partner position.
3. Underarm Turn Right commences with weight on left foot in closed position, facing diagonal center,
Measure 1, forward half of natural turn,
Measure 2, back half of natural turn leading Funder arm turn right. Figure may be preceded with a left foot forward change and followed with a right foot forward progressive change.
4. Underarm Turn Left begins closed position facing diagonal wall or line of dance,
Measure 1 forward half of reverse turn,
Measure 2 back half of a reverse turn with lead for Funder arm turn left.
5. Progressive Fifth Position Breaks begins closed position facing line of dance,
Measure 1, left foot forward and point leading follower's 5th position break to left,

Measure 2, right foot forward balance point leading follower's 5th position break to R. Strong shape away from partner on count 2 of each measure.

6. Spot Turn Combination commences in closed position facing diagonal wall or line of dance,

Measure 1, left foot forward progressive change,

Measure 2, right foot side, open break,

Measure 3 back spot turn to right,

Measure 4 forward spot turn to right,

Measure 5, back spot turn to right,

Measure 6, right foot side and 5th position break.

Steps Measure 3 through Measure 5 are referred to as Natural Fleckerls in International Viennese Waltz.

7. Reverse Underarm Turn commence in left side partner facing wall,

Measure 1, 3 steps circling right to prepare for Funder arm turn left,

Measure 2 is right foot forward twinkle leading Funder arm turn left ending in left side partner. The figure maybe proceeded with steps 1-12 of figure 5B from Bronze VW (cross body lead with under arm turn). If ended facing new line of dance, this figure may be followed by figure 6 from Bronze VW (hand-to-hand).

8. Advanced Hand-to-hand Combination commences in left side partner facing line of dance,

Measure 1, face to face with cross behind,

Measure 2 forward runs in left side partner,

Measure 3, face to face with cross behind,

Measure 4, free spin to right,

Measure 5 left foot forward canter run (follower's canter free spin),

Measure 6, left foot forward canter run, (follower's canter free spin to left outside position),

Measure 7, left foot forward check (follower's left outside position),

Measure 8, back half of reverse turn from left outside position (under turned). Measure 8 can use a left foot forward progressive change step to eliminate turn if needed. Follower's canter free spins to the right may alternatively be danced as under arm canter turns.

9. Standing Spin commences with weight on left foot in left outside position in double hand hold backing diagonal wall against line of dance,

Measure 1, right foot back twinkle from left outside partner to facing partner, commence leading under arm turn left,

Measure 2, Canter run circling right (follower's canter turn L),

Measure 3, paddle turn right in right outside partner position,

Measure 4 Paddle turn right in right outside partner,

Measure 5 is the back half of natural turn. Right outside partner in this figure is danced with leader's right hand on follower's left shoulder blade and follower's right hand on top of leader's left shoulder and each extending their left arms out to the side. Steps in Measure 3 and 4 are referred to a paddle turn. Follow this figure with a right foot forward progressive change. Alternative ending for the last measure is to use steps 7-12 of figure 10 (Open Right Turn)

10. Open Right Turn begins closed position facing diagonal wall,
Measure 1, Twinkle open,
Measure 2, leader's passing right turn changing hold to right outside partner,
Measure 3, back half of open right turn,
Measure 4, Forward half of open right turn,
Measure 5 back half of natural turn from right outside partner to closed position. Right outside partner in this figure is danced with leader's right hand on follower's left shoulder blade and Follower's right hand on top of leader's left shoulder and each extending their left arms out to the side

Viennese Waltz -International

Bronze

1. Natural Turn begins closed position facing diagonal center,
Measure 1, 1/8 right turn, right foot forward, 1/4 right turn, left foot side, 1/8 right turn, right foot closes to left foot,
Measure 2, 1/8 right turn, left foot back and slightly side, 3/8 right turn, right foot side, left foot closes to right foot. Figure ends facing diagonal center. Turn can be reduced ¼ overall to navigate corners in line of dance. This is called a right turn in American.

2. Right Foot Forward Closed Change begins right foot forward, left foot diagonally forward left side leading, right foot closes to left foot. Like the second Measure of a Waltz progressive

3. Reverse Turn begins closed position facing diagonal wall,
Measure 1, 1/8 left turn, left foot forward, 1/4 turn, right foot side and slightly back, 1/8 turn, left foot crosses in front of right foot,
Measure 2, 1/8 left turn, right foot back and slightly side, 3/8 left turn, left foot side, right foot closes to left foot. Figure ends facing diagonal wall. Turn can be increased ¼ overall to navigate corners in the line of dance.

4. Left foot Forward Closed Change begins closed position facing line of dance, left foot forward, right foot diagonally forward right side leading, left foot closes to right foot. Like first half of a Waltz box.

Silver

5. Right Foot Backward Closed Change begins closed position, right foot back, left foot diagonally back left side leading, right foot closes to left foot. Like the second half of a Waltz box.

6. Left foot Backward Closed Change begins closed position, left foot back, right foot diagonally back right-side lead, left foot closes to right foot.

Quick Step

Quick Step uses the same frame as Waltz and Foxtrot. The music is much faster, so there is very little rise and fall.

Quick Step Bronze Figures
1A. Quarter Turn to Right begins closed position facing diagonal wall, SQQS, right foot forward, 1/8 right turn, left foot to side, 1/8 right turn, right foot closes to left foot, left foot to side and slightly back. Figure ends Backing diagonal center.
1B. Quarter Turn to Left begins closed position facing diagonal center, SQQ, right foot back, left foot closes toward right foot (heel pivot), ¼ left turn, left foot closes to right foot w/o weight. Figure ends facing diagonal wall.
2. Progressive Chassé begins closed position Backing diagonal center, SQQS, right foot back, ¼ left turn, left foot side, right foot closes to left foot, left foot to side and slightly back. Figure ends facing diagonal wall.
3. Forward Lock Step begins outside partner facing diagonal wall, SQQS, right foot forward in CBMP, left foot to side, right foot crosses behind left foot, left foot diagonal forward. Figure ends facing diagonal wall.
4. Natural Turn with Hesitation begins closed position facing diagonal wall, SQQSSS, right foot forward, ¼ right turn, left foot to side, 1/8 right turn, right foot closes to left foot, left foot back, 3/8 right turn, right foot to side small step (heel pull), left foot closes to right foot w/o weight. Figure ends facing diagonal center.
5. Progressive Chassé to Right begins closed position facing diagonal center, SQQS, left foot forward, 1/8 left turn, right foot to side, 1/8 left turn, left foot closes to right foot, right foot to side and slightly back. Figure ends backing diagonal wall.
6. Back Lock begins closed position Backing diagonal wall, SQQS, left foot back in CBMP, right foot back, left foot crosses in front of right foot, right foot diagonal back. ends backing center or wall.
7. Running Finish begins closed position backing diagonal wall, QQS, left foot back in CBMP, 3/8 right turn, right foot to side and slightly back, left foot forward preparing to step OP left side leading. Figure ends facing line of dance.
8. Natural Spin Turn begins closed position facing diagonal wall, SQQSSS, right foot forward, 3/8 right turn, left foot side, right foot closes to left foot, left foot back ½ turn to right, right foot held in CBMP (a pivot), right foot forward in CBMP continuing the right turn, 3/8 turn, left foot to the side and slightly back Figure ends backing diagonal center. Amounts of turn can vary to create other alignments.

9. Natural Turn and Back Lock begins closed position facing diagonal wall, SQQ SQQS, right foot forward, ¼ right turn, left foot side, right foot closes to left foot, left foot back, right foot back right-side lead, left foot crosses in front of right foot, right foot diagonally back. Figure ends B line of dance.

10. Tipple Chassé to Right at a Corner begins closed position backing line of dance, SQQ SQQS, left foot back, ¼ right turn, right foot to side, left foot closes to right foot, 1/8 right turn, right foot to side and slightly back, left foot diagonal forward left side leading, right foot crosses behind left foot, left foot diagonally forward prep for outside partner. Figure ends facing diagonal wall.

11. Double Reverse Spin begins facing line of dance, SSQQ, left foot forward beginning to turn, 3/8 turn L, right foot to side, ½ turn, left foot closes to right foot w/o weight (Toe Pivot). Amount turn and directions may vary.

12. Chassé Reverse Turn begins closed position facing line of dance, SQQ, left foot forward, ¼ left turn, right foot to side, 1/8 left turn, left foot closes to right foot. Figure ends backing line of dance.

13. Natural Pivot Turn begins closed position facing diagonal wall, SQQS, right foot forward, ¼ right turn, left foot to side, 1/8 left turn, right foot closes to left foot, left foot back (right foot held in CBMP) with ½ right turn (a pivot). Figure ends facing line of dance.

14. Closed Impetus begins backing line of dance, SSSS, left foot back beg turn to R, 3/8 turn, right foot closes to left foot (heel turn), ¼ turn, left foot side and slightly back

15. Reverse Pivot begins backing line of dance right foot, This figure is just a S or an & count. Back in CBMP small step turning up to ½ turn to left, left foot held in CBMP.

Quick Step Silver Figures

16. V-6 begins closed position, backing diagonal center, SQQSQQ, left foot back, right foot back right side leading, left foot crosses in front of right foot (lock step), right foot back, left foot back in CBMP, right foot back, ¼ turn left, Left foot side and slightly forward. Figure ends diagonal wall.

17. Quick Open Reverse begins closed position, line of dance, SQQ, left foot forward, 3/8 turn left, right foot side, 1/8 turn left, left foot back in CBMP. Figure ends backing line of dance. Alignments may vary.

18. Four Quick Run begins closed position, backing line of dance, SQQQQS, right foot back, 3/8 turn left, left foot side and slightly forward, right foot forward in CBMP OP, left foot diagonal forward, right foot crosses behind left foot, left foot diagonal forward. Figure ends diagonal wall.

19. Running Right Turn begins closed position, diagonal wall, SQQ SSSS QQS, right foot forward, ¼ turn right, left foot side, 1/8 turn right, left foot back turned in (ugly foot) with ½ turn to right (pivot), right foot forward in CBMP continuing to turn, left foot side with 3/8 turn right, right foot back right side leading with 1/8 turn right, left foot back in CBMP continuing to turn, right foot side and slightly forward with ¼ turn right, left foot forward preparing to step OP left side leading. Figure ends line of dance. Other alignments can be used.

20. Cross Swivel begins closed position, diagonal wall, SS, left foot forward, ¼ turn L, right foot almost closes to left foot slightly back without weight. Figure ends diagonal center. Note that the following step will be right foot forward in CBMP OP.

21. Fish Tail begins closed position, diagonal center, SQQQQS, right foot forward in CBMP OP (as previous figure ended), 1/8 turn right, left foot crosses behind right foot, 1/8 turn right, right foot forward and slightly to the side small step, left foot diagonally forward left side lead, right foot crosses behind left foot, left foot diagonally forward. Fish tail may also be danced diagonal wall with no turn.

22. Tipple Chassé to Left begins outside partner facing diagonal wall, SQQS, right foot forward in CBMP OP, ¼ turn right, left foot side, 1/8 turn right, right foot closes to left foot, left foot side and slightly back. Figure ends backing line of dance.

23. Closed Telemark begins closed position, diagonal center, SSS, left foot forward beginning turn to left, right foot side turning 3/8 left, left foot side and slightly forward turning 3/8 left. Figure ends diagonal wall

Peabody

The Peabody is the predecessor to the Quick Step. Peabody is danced to very fast big band music. Frame is a little more up right than normal foxtrot or waltz. The dance should glide along the floor with limited raise and fall.

Syllabus (all figures start with the left foot)

1. Basic Right Eight Count Turn begins closed position diagonal wall, All slows, forward, forward, side, back, back, side, forward, forward. Figure ends diagonal center

2. Basic Left Eight Count Turn begins closed position diagonal center, All slows, forward, forward, forward, side, back OSP, back, side, forward OPS. CBMP used on forward steps. Figure ends diagonal wall

3. Quick Count Run begins closed position line of dance or curving, SSQQ, SSQQ, FFFF, facing side close. The quick steps are on the balls of the feet.

4. Lock Steps Forward and Back begins closed position diagonal wall, SS QQS SSSS QQS SSSS, two forward steps, forward lock steps OSP, a forward step and ½ right turn in frame, back lock steps OSP, a back step and ½ right turn in frame. Figure ends diagonal center

5. Right Underarm Turn begins closed position diagonal wall, SS forward steps, QQS side close & slightly back prep for outside under arm turn right, SQQS back side closed side leading two outside under arm turn right, SQQ across side closed. Figure ends diagonal wall

6. Left Underarm Turn begins closed position diagonal center, SSS forward side back making ½ turn left, SQQ back side across while leading an inside under arm turn left making ¼ turn left following partner's turn, SS FF. Figure ends diagonal wall.

7. Progressive Swivels with Underarm Turn begins closed position diagonal center, SSSS forward side back (going to two hand open position) back, QQSS QQSS all back while follower does swivels (turning both feet out the same direction at the same time) lead by turning the back in the direction of the swivel, SS back side (turning ½ turn right), SSSS FFF facing while follower makes two under arm turns right, SS F facing in closed position.

8. Right Pivots begins closed position diagonal wall around the corner to diagonal wall new line of dance, all slows, FFSB with ½ turn right to be backing line of dance, three pivots (back and side, pivot, forward, keeping knees flexed), side back stops the pivoting, side OSP, FF facing going back in line.

9. Forward and Back Twinkles begins closed position line of dance, all SQQ, three forward twinkles, right turn, three backward twinkles, left turn. The twinkles are danced with passing feet. Figure ends diagonal wall

10. Offset Grapevine with Skip begins closed position diagonal wall, SS FF, 8Q grapevine SBSFSBSF, SS skip, skip, FF. Grapevine is danced with limited rise and fall. The change of direction in the grapevine is accomplished by a swiveling of the feet as opposed to a crossing over of the feet. The skip should include a bit of hip pull back to avoid bumping knees. Figure ends diagonal wall

11. Promenade Grapevine with Hook Turn begins closed position diagonal wall, SQQ twinkle to promenade position, 8Q grapevine, SSSS forward and across in promenade position, side, hook behind, full turn to the right for both partners. The turn is done on the ball right foot and the heel of the left foot keeping the knees flexed to remain upright in the turn. Figure ends wall.

12. Fallaway Grapevine begins closed position diagonal wall, 4S FFSB turning to back line of dance in Fallaway position, 8Q grapevine, SQQ BSC turning, SQQ FSC twinkle to promenade position. Figure ends closed position diagonal center

13. Spot Grapevine with Underarm Turn begins closed position, 4S FFSB turning to back line of dance, 8Q back spot turn turning right (spot turn uses a paddle turn where one foot pivots in place while the other foot pushes around to create the turn) while partner's action is like a curving grapevine, 4S outside under arm turn right for partner while continuing to turn right, 8Q back spot turn turning right, 4S BSCS with inside under arm turn left for partner.

14. Promenade to Counter Promenade Runs begins closed position diagonal wall, SQQ twinkle to promenade position, SQQ right turn ½ to counter promenade position, SQQ right turn ½ to promenade position, SQQ right turn ½ to closed position, SQQ right turn ½ to Fallaway position, 8Q grapevine, SS side then bring LR to right foot no weight.

15. Open Right Turn to Man & Lady's Underarm Turns begins closed position diagonal wall, the first three Measures are an open right turn from waltz or foxtrot [SQQ twinkle to promenade position, SQQ (right foot forward and across, side, back), SQQ BCS with heel turn on the close], SSSS FBFB under arm turn right making two full turns for leader, QQS SCS while leading under arm turn right for partner. Figure ends diagonal center

Rhythm and Latin

Frame

The closed position frame is a bit more relaxed than Smooth. The partners align squared to each other instead of right front to right front in smooth. Both partners will be carrying their weight **on the forward part of the foot**, even leaning forward a bit. The tone in the frame **is a push connection towards each other** instead of the smooth pull connection away from each other. Leader indicates his direction of his movement with his **hips and ribcage**.

A common frame for many rhythm figures is a one hand hold. Usually this is leader's left hand to follower' right hand, but it can be any combination. The key to communication with the one hand hold is to maintain good tone in the arm all the way into the core of the body. Keep the elbow bent. Keep the hands in the common center with a **slight push into the connection**.

Footwork

Feet should be slightly turned out and kept in contact with the floor using slight foot pressure. Footwork is generally ball flat throughout however there are exceptions. Most of the movement stays on the ball of the foot.

Movement

The basic movement is very different from the Smooth dances. **The rib cage moves first and the foot moves to support the body in its new position.** The foot should be moved quickly. The weight should stay on the standing leg as long as possible while the hips and core are **wound up (stretched against the next movement)** so that when they are released, a quick movement result. Weight changes should be made on the beat. Turns should be made using the **wind up and release** to make a quick, sharp turn.

Use **Cuban Motion**, stepping with a flexed knee on to the ball of the receiving foot and delaying the straightening of the leg. Keep chest lifted and move the ribcage in opposition to the hips. Take small steps. Lead and follow from the center of the body, using compression and leverage. Keep the free arm alive by moving the arms in a natural way that expresses the music. **The movement of the arms should be initiated by the movement of the core of the body**.

When I first saw the professional dancers move with lots of hip action, I thought that it was some sort of allusion, like a magic trick. I discovered that these dancers had control over muscles that I did not even know I had. I went to the gym and started to use the Rotary Torso machine to strengthen and stretch my core muscles. After a few months, I could rotate my hips around, but as soon as I demonstrated this ability, more actions were assigned. Next, I was asked to raise and lower the hip as it rotated. More muscles to train. It is very important at this point to remember **that for each action in one direction there needs to be an offsetting stretch in the other direction by another part of the body to maintain balance**.

Changes of direction are made with sharp turns around the standing leg and settling to move in the new direction. This is done by **closing the feet (bringing them together and changing weight)** then settling to turn and then move. **Settling means: sending the hip of the standing leg forward and around to the side around and back to provide the power for forward movement** as an example. This is called Cuban Motion. Think of this as **"Step, Hip, Step, Hip"**. This action applies in changes of direction and turns. Change of direction takes place during the **hip action**. This hip action can be performed as a **figure 8 rolling motion** described above or with more of a back and forth **popping action** with only a slight rolling motion. Varying these actions will create a more interesting overall look.

Rumba, Cha Cha, Mambo and Salsa have many figures that use a **checking action** when changing direction, i.e., a movement forward and then replace back. The check is a step that only takes a percentage of weight instead of a full change of weight in a normal step. The check step is taken, the hip action is completed and the weight is returned to the previous sending leg which has not moved. By not transferring all of the weight, the action can be greater and the movement will appear to be faster. Many figures begin with or include a check. There is a more detailed description of a check on the next page. Be sure to turn out the foot on the checking action.

The other action that is often used to start a figure is an **open break**. An open break is sort of like a check, only the lead is for partner to take a step back while the leader also takes a step back. This action opens up the partners for the figure that follows.

The movement for back steps is a bit different, the foot moves into position first and the hip follows with the body staying relatively forward.

A check is used in many places. For example, a check is a part of the basic in Cha Cha, as the beginning of a cross over break after a quarter turn, or as the start of a cross body lead. A check starts with a forward step as described above however only a percentage (say 50%) of the weight is moved to the left leg.
On the next count change from a left side lead to a right-side lead in the upper body and flex the right knee forward, leaving the toe of the right foot in place.
On the next count, while maintaining the right-side lead, replace the weight back onto the right foot. This positioning puts you in wound up (CBMP) position for a step or chasse to the left or a turn to the left.

Movement for the more advanced dancer

The starting position for movement is the weight on one leg, with the foot, knee, hip and sternum in a straight line. The other foot will have the heal raised and the hip will be lifted. You should think of this as the neutral position for all dances. Try to begin and **end** each measure in this position. Releasing the hip of the standing leg will provide power to create faster foot movement. Learning to end each movement in this position takes a lot of practice, think of it as "leaving a little gas in the tank" to start the next movement. **This is one of the biggest nuggets in the book.** The right hip held under the sternum, will feel as if you have stopped in mid motion, but you must not allow the hip to swing through as you need to swing for the next actions. This saving of swing allows the hip to swing through to the other side with Cuban motion to move the left foot. Settle the right hip (move the hip back) to bring the left foot in, settle the right hip more while moving the left foot forward. See why you needed to have saved some swing or settle and not used it all in the beginning. Now the weight moves to the left foot. The left foot, left hip and head aligned winding up for the next movement. One heel is always up. This action will create a constant movement of the hips in a figure eight motion with a raising and lowering of the free hip. This winding up and releasing of the hips will increase foot speed. Think of this action as Step, Hip, Step, Hip.

Turning in Rhythm and Latin dances

Turn is created by rotation within the standing leg from the ankle through the hip. Keep sternum over the standing leg then move the sternum to the new standing leg. To get more rotation than you can get from within the standing leg, place the foot of the standing leg for the turn angled in the direction of the turn. The turnout should **start at the foot and include turnout in the hip** to get maximum rotation. This is sort of a foot windup needs to be anticipated when stepping on to the leg that will be creating the turn. Same for the ladies executing under arm turns.

If the turn requires more rotation than can be created from the turning in the foot and leg, the momentum from the turning action is continued by the ball of the foot rotating on the floor. Additional momentum can be **gained for a turn or spin from a wind up of the top in advance of the turn** to be released to assist with rotation at the end of the turn. Think about making the top rotate even more than the feet. **The free arm should be up at shoulder height or higher and be used as part of the wind up and release to create additional momentum**. Using the arm in this way is natural and will assist in making the turn look effortless as well as coordinating the movement of the arm into the movement of the body

When going backwards in rotation, the bottom (the feet to the hips) goes first. When going forward in rotation, the top (sternum to belly bottom) goes first. Left turning figures normally will have a left side lead in preparation for the turn. Right turning figures normally will have a right-side lead in preparation for the turn.

When "in CBMP" is listed in the figure, the side leads will be opposite i.e., left foot forward in CBMP would mean that the right hip through shoulder would be ahead of the left with the left foot going forward, creating a windup in the core. CBMP is the abbreviation for Contra Body Movement or Position.

Leading Under Arm Turns

In order to be a good leader of turns for partner, the leader must know the type of turn that partner will be doing. The raising the of the arm in the direction of the turn is the same as smooth, but the turning actions are done on & counts between the steps. The most common under arm turn is a two-step turn which is lead when stepping back on leader's right foot. The lead brings partner forward to put weight on her left leg. Leader settles which lead partner to turn to the right 180 degrees around her standing leg. Leader then leads partner forward to her right leg. The leader again settles which leads partner to complete the turn.

If a turn is lead going to the side (as in a side chasse in Cha Cha), partner may need to do a three step turn in which the turn is done rotating 360 around the first standing leg with a closing step and a side step to finish. The leader needs to recognize that the follower with need all of the rotation on the first step (without side movement) and then finish with side movement. If the leader moves to the side before the rotation is completed, follower will be pulled off balance.

Cha Cha

Cha Cha (perhaps more correctly called Cha Cha Cha) is lively and fun. Unlike the smooth dances which travel around the line of dance, Cha Cha is a spot dance that emphasizes Cuban Motion and rhythm expressed throughout the body. In Cha Cha the feet move quickly from place to place and the hips and ribcage fill the music with constant motion.

Due to the speed of Cha Cha, Cuban Motion is less pronounced than in Rumba, especially on counts 4&, as these steps represent only half a beat. Standard rhythm in Cha Cha is 1234& or more appropriately phased 234&1. Alternate rhythms of 1234, 2&34&1 and 1&2&3&4& are also used in some figures. A more dynamic movement is created by emphasizing count 1 and sizing the chasse steps as "small, small, medium." Body movement should interpret the staccato feeling of the music. The weight of the body should be over the center of the standing foot with energy moving toward your partner to create connection (weight forward). Maintain same height throughout the dance, keeping the spine long, the head up and the shoulders down. Initiate the movement from the rib cage, but do not allow the shoulders to tilt from side to side.

Walks, rocks or checks are generally danced on the 2 3. These actions can be forward or back walks. The walks can be a regular walk or a delayed walk. The delayed forward walk can be danced on a straight leg or a bent leg. Delayed back walks are on a straight leg. The 2 3 can also be used in a forward walk turning, such as when a follower is doing a Crossbody lead.

Split weight actions are used for a change of direction. Examples are checks and back rocks. **Cucarachas are also a split weight action that can be used in the place of a back rock**. **A check** by the leader is to step forward with **partial weight** followed by replacing the weight to the other foot. The follower mimics this action with a matching back rock. An **open break** is a similar action where the leader gives pressure in the connection for the follower to rock back like a check, while the leader also rocks back.

Cucarachas is a step to the side bringing the hips forward and around followed be a similar action to the other side, creating a figure 8 action with the hips. A Cucarachas is done on two flat feet. Cucarachas can sometimes be used in place of a back rock in Crossbody leads and while leading under arm turns.

Cha Cha is said to **"break on the two"** meaning the change of direction step takes place on the second beat. In International Cha Cha, Mambo, International Rumba and sometimes Salsa also break on the two. An International Cha Cha basic starts with a forward check on the 2.

A chasse is a series of steps chasing themselves and chasses are used in Cha Cha for the movements that are commonly danced of the 4&1. When we first learn Cha Cha the three steps of a Chasse are divided equally over the 4&1, **as we gain experience, <u>we dance the first two steps of the chasse on ½ beats and use a full beat for the last step to emphasize the 1 beat in the music</u>**. Most chasses can be started with either foot. The advanced dancers will sometimes stretch the 3 and then dance the 4 & even more quickly to create an interesting speed variation within the measure to emphasize the various beats. Think of the "&" count as speeding up the count preceding it.

Chassé, French for 'to chase', is a dance term used in many dances. All variations are triple-steps in a "step-together-step" pattern. The following is a list of the Cha Cha chasses:

Side chasse is left foot to side, right foot closes to left foot, left foot to side or right foot side, left foot closes to right foot, right foot side.
Forward chasse is forward, other foot beside slightly back, forward.
Back chasse is back, other foot beside slightly back, back.
In place chasse or compact chasse, is the bending and straightening of the legs in place.
Forward lock is forward, other foot crosses behind toe turned out, forward. *See detail below.*
Back lock is back, other foot crosses in front first foot, then back.
Forward run is forward, forward, forward.
Back run is back, back, back.
Twist chasse is right foot back, replace weight to left foot, right foot forward and across to the toe delayed action, left foot closes to right foot turning to the right, right foot side.
Slip chasse is back with slipping action, forward, replace.
Ronda chasse is left foot forward, replace weight to right foot, left foot back with ronde action which is circling the foot around to the side and then behind the right foot, right foot closes to left foot, left foot to the side.

These terms will be used to shorten the description of the dance figures in this section.
In general, the forward lock step is a strong push off the right leg, a strong pulling of the hips forward with the core as the right foot moves behind the left and another strong push of the right leg starting a new lock.

Again, for the more advanced dancer, the detail for the movement in the **forward lock** step described with the counts &e4e&a1 is:

&) Make a diamond with the left leg (bring the left knee up, raising the ankle with the toe on the floor beside the right foot, settling in the right hip by bringing it up and back).

4) Place the left foot forward on to ball then flat.

e) Move the weight of the left hip on to the left leg continuing to turn out the right foot.

&) Bring the right foot forward behind the left foot in a Latin cross position using the core to pull the foot forward staying on the ball. The knees should be bent at this point.

a) Settle the right hip making a diamond.

1) Push forward from the right leg for a step on the left foot on the two original tracks.

Start again on & for the right leg to continue forward locks.

Again, for the more advanced dancers, in general a back lock is a step back, a pulling back of the hip which also rotates back pulling the other foot to lock in front and step back. The detail for the back-lock step described with the counts &4e&a1 is:

&) Make a diamond with the right leg bring the right knee up, raising the ankle with the toe on the floor beside the left foot, settling in the left hip.

4) Place the right foot back and slightly left on the toe.

e) Roll the right hip back and on to the ball of the right foot while increasing the turn-out of the right foot.

&) Continue to rolling the right hip back pulling the left foot back in front and slightly across of the right foot on the ball creating a Latin cross position; the knees should be bent.

a) Make a diamond with the right leg, settling the left hip.

1) Step back with the hips square on the two original tracks.

Start again on & for the left leg to continue to back locks.

For the purposes of describing the figures more concisely, the measures in the summary may not be true musical measures. Instead, they may represent a practical grouping of the steps and count, 234&1 as an example. Some figures may be blended by eliminating the last measures of one figure and go right into the second measures of the next figure. Most steps in Cha Cha have a chasse danced on the 4&1. Sometimes a chasse is added on the 2&3.

Cha Cha Bronze American

1. **Basic in Place** 1st half, 1234& left foot side, right foot back, replace weight to left foot, right foot closes to left foot, Replace weight to left foot, 2nd half, 1234& replace weight to right foot, left foot forward, Replace weight to right foot, left foot closes to right foot, Replace weight to right foot.
2. **Side Basic** 1st half, 1234&1, left foot side, right foot back, replace weight to left foot, Side chasse right left right, 2nd half, 234&1* left foot forward, replace weight to right foot, left foot side chasse. *The extra 1 count is added to complete the chasses, which is the natural action.*
3. **Progressive Basic** 1st half, 1234&1, left foot side, right foot back, replace weight to left foot, forward run RLR, 2nd half, 234&1*, left foot forward, replace weight to right foot, back run left, right left.
4. **Outside Partner** 1st measure is left foot side, right foot forward break in right outside partner, right foot side chasse. The 2nd measure is left foot forward break in left outside position, left foot side chasse. The relative position of the partners needs to be strongly led from the top.
5. **Crossover Break** 1st Measure, 1st half of side basic ending in prep left side partner, 2nd Measure, left foot crossover break (rotate ¼ to right on standing right leg, left foot forward with small weight, right knee checks to left, replace weight to right leg and rotate ¼ to left), left foot side chasse, 3rd Measure, right foot cross over break, right foot chasse, 4th Measure left foot crossover break, left foot side chasse, 5th Measure, solo spot turn on 2 3, 6th Measure, 2nd half of side basic.
6. **Cross Body Lead** 1234&1, first half of Side Basic, 234&1, first half of cross-body lead (left foot forward, replace weight to right foot 1/8 left turn, left side chasse with 1/8 left turn, lead partner for a forward run or forward walk turning), 234&1, 2nd half of cross body lead (right foot back off track, ¼ left turn, left foot forward, right foot forward run or right foot side chasse right left right, lead partner as needed), 234&1, 2nd half of side basic. Three-step under arm turns can be added to the side chasses.
7. **Open Break Underarm Turn** 1st Measure, first half of side basic, 2 Measure, first half of cross body lead, 3rd Measure, second half of cross body lead with side chasse to facing position, 4th Measure, 234&1, open break, left foot side chasse (left foot back{leading partner back}, replace to right foot, left side chasse), 5th Measure, 234&1, right foot 5th position break (follower's spot under arm turn right), right side chasse, 6th Measure, 234&1, 2nd half of side basic.
8. **Chase Turn** 1st Measure, first part of progressive basic, 2nd Measure, left foot forward chase turn ½ turn right, left foot forward run, 3rd Measure, right foot forward chase turn ½ turn left, right foot forward run, 4th Measure, left right forward chase turn, ½ turn right, left foot turning chasse, ½ turn to R, 5th Measure,

right foot back break, right foot forward run follower's full chase turn, 6th Measure, 2nd half of side basic.

9. Shoulder Check Side basic ending in facing position, open break with left foot side chasse turning right while follower does under arm turn left with the leader stopping the turn after ½ turn by placing the right hand on partner's shoulder blade, right foot check forward in front of partner then right foot side chasse turning left while partner does under arm turn right, 2nd half of side basic. This figure is commonly done with two consecutive shoulder checks before finishing.

10. Shadow Positions or **Shadow Cross Body Leads**. From a right-to-right hand hold, a cross body lead to end in left side shadow position over 3 Measures.

Starts with a forward break on the 2, replace on the 3, turn left ¼ turn and chasse on the 4&1 while partner does a forward lock, lead partner to left (partner does a forward walk turning) while leader rocks back and replaces on the 23, chasse to the right on 4&1, left foot crossover break in left shadow position on 2, replace on 3, turn to facing position with chasse to the left on 4&1.

This can be repeated again with the difference that you are now in facing position with partner and she needs to be turned ¼ turn to the right to do a forward walk turning on the 2 3 of the cross-body lead. Then turn to facing position chasse to the right on 4&1, then a left foot cross over break in left shadow position then turn ¼ left and left side chasse, right foot 5th position break with under arm turn right for partner, 2nd half of side basic.

This figure can be made more interesting by adding three step turns into some or all of the chasses.

11. Butterfly 1st half of side basic ending in left side partner, left foot cross over break and left foot side chasse, right foot back break in left side partner then right foot chasse, left foot crossover break then left side chasse, right foot 5th position break while follower does a spot under arm turn right then right foot chasse, 2nd half of basic.

12. Alternating Underarm Turns 1st half of side basic ending facing in double hand hold, open break in double hand hold left foot side chasse in double hand hold, right foot 5th position break with follower's spot under arm turn right and right foot side chasse in double hand hold, leader spot under arm turn right and left foot side chasse in double hand hold, right foot 5th position break while partner does under arm turn right then right foot side chasse, 2nd half of side basic.

13. Crossbody Pull Back 1st half of side basic, left foot forward break then left foot side break and close while follower does a forward check and pull back, 2nd half of Crossbody lead, 2nd half of side basic.

14. Three Cha Chas back on 23 then right foot forward lock, left foot forward lock on 2&3, right foot forward lock, forward check on 23 then right foot back lock, left foot back lock on 2&3, right foot back lock, right foot back break then right foot forward run, 2nd half of side basic. A slight rotation of the upper body is recommended, changing with each lock into the direction of the lock, i.e. right-side lead for right foot forward lock. The locks can be done in Double hand hold or in alternating hand hold with the forward shoulder arm connecting to partner's same hand. When using alternating hand hold, the off arm should be stretched to out to the side, up and back.

15. Crossover Flick to Side Break Crossover break to right (left foot crossover break) and left chasse, ¼ turn to left then right foot forward left foot forward and slightly across to pivot ½ turn right the left foot then right foot back lock, ¼ turn to left then left foot side and flick replace weight to right foot ¼ turn right and then left foot forward lock, ¼ turn to the left then right foot side break and right foot chasse in place, 2nd half of side basic.

Cha Cha Bronze Variations

1. Fifth Position Breaks (Rumba) is the rumba figure with a side chasse between the 5th position breaks instead of the slow count.
2. Crossover and Side Rocks (Rumba) is the rumba figure with a forward lock after the crossover break and a side chasse added to the side rocks.
3. Open Rumba Walks (Rumba) is like rumba with cha cha timing.
4. Cradle Circle (Rumba) is like rumba with cha cha timing.
5. Open Circular Walks (Rumba) is Circular walks in hammerlock position. Just like rumba with cha cha timing.
6. Spot Turn Combination (Rumba) is the rumba with cha cha timing.
7. Check and Circular Walk (Bolero) is bolero with cha cha timing.
8. Crossbody Lead with Inside Turn (Mambo) is mambo with cha cha timing.
9. Back Spot Turn (Mambo) is the mambo with cha cha timing, from open break.
10. Forward Spot to Surprise (Mambo) is the mambo with cha cha timing.
11. Crossover Swivels and Pullback (Mambo) is the crossover break, replacing the chasse after the crossover with three swivels and a pullback.

Cha Cha American Silver

1. Cross-Over Flick Combination is the back half of a side basic (chasse' to the right), cross over (turn right on the right leg, check with the left, replace weight onto the right, rotate to the left, place weight on the left and flick to the right). A flick is to hold the leg and foot out with no weight instead of closing the feet. Cross over and flick to the right again, cross over to triple to left, grapevine lock, back step to side flick and cross over, ends with a side basic with follower's under arm turn.

2. Back Spot Turn with Quick Underarm Turn is the back half of a side basic, open break to back spot turn, back spot turn with follower's under arm turn left, open break to back spot turn, back spot turn with follower's under arm turn left, crossover break to triple left, side basic with lady's checked under arm turn right then under arm turn left, forward half of side basic.

3. Pullback Grapevine back half of side basic, side break turning left, grapevine to the left, side break and grapevine to the right, side break and grapevine to the left, side break and grapevine to the right, side break and basic in place, side basic to the right then side basic to the left 12&34&1, forward half of side basic.

4. Cross Body, Surprise, Quick Turn back half of side basic, cross body lead, side break to cross body lead, left foot opposition check to side break (Lady dances side break to quick under arm turn left), side basic, side basic.

5. Pullback Combination back half of side basic (lady breaks OP on man's left side then under arm turn left ending in cradle position, left foot back break to left foot forward break (lady dances right foot back break to under arm turn right), pull back, forward walk to pull back and forward break (lady dances pull back to quick under arm turn left to pull back forward break), close and two triples to the left.

6. Open Turn, Wrap & Syncopation back half of side basic, open break to back spot turn (lady dances open break to under arm turn left), back walks to side break (lady walks forward), solo spot turn left in front of lady and syncopated fifth position breaks, cross body lead, forward half of side basic.

7. Cross Over, Twist & Fan is the back half of side basic, cross over break promenade run, back lock to quick side break 12&3a4&1, fan to side triple.

8. Forward and Back Syncopation is the back half of side basic, full triple to right with back lock (lady dances back break to forward lock), back half of side basic, (lady turns under arm turn right), step side to syncopated forward and back breaks, step back to syncopated forward and back breaks, forward half of basic.

9. Across the Back is the back half of basic, open break to side break (lady dances open break to forward walks behind man's right side, right foot back break to basic in place (lady dances left foot forward break on man's left side then grapevine back to man's right side), left foot back break to left foot cross break (lady dances right foot forward break on man's right side then grapevine back to man's left side, back spot turn, forward half of side basic.

10. Syncopated Cross-Over Variation is the back half of basic, quick left foot cross over and quick right foot cross over 12&34&1, double quick left foot cross over break to side triple left 12&34&1, right foot cross check to ronde, left foot cross over break to quick solo spin to left, forward half of side basic.

11. Turkish Towel (from International Gold syllabus) starts in right-to-right hand hold with a left foot forward check. After replacing from the check, do an in-place chasse bring partner in close, on count 2 right foot back step lead partner to an outside turn and make ¼ turn to left to be in front of partner and chasse to the right in front of partner as partner chasses to the left behind you. On the next 2 count break back while partner breaks forward, chasse and repeat. After two sets, spin partner out and reconnect.

International Cha Cha Bronze

1. Basic Movement Forward half of basic: left foot forward on the 2, replace weight to right foot on 3, left foot to side and slightly back, right foot closes to left foot, left foot side on the 4&1, a side chasse.
Back half of basic: right foot back on the 2, replace weight to left foot on the 3, right side chasse.

2. New Yorkers Same as American cross over breaks.

4. Shoulder to Shoulder Same as American outside partner.

5. Hand-to-hand left foot back in fallaway position (5th position) maintaining right to left hand hold, replace, side chasse, right foot back in Fallaway position maintaining left-to-right hand hold.

6. The Three Cha Cha Chas from a back break, three consecutive forward locks 4&1 2&3 4&1, forward break to change direction and three consecutive back locks 4&1 2&3 4&1 in Double hand hold with sides leading the locking actions. Alternating right-to-right and left to left hand hold may also be used.

7. Side Steps left foot to side, close right foot to left foot, left foot side chasse, and back to the right, right foot to side, close left foot to right foot, right foot side chasse.

8. There and Back close left foot to right foot, replace weight to right foot, three small back steps (backward runs), and back, right foot back, transfer weight to left foot, three small forward steps (forward runs).

9. Time Steps Left foot time step: left foot behind right foot, replace weight to right foot, left foot side chasse, right foot time step: right foot behind left foot, replace weight to left foot, right foot side chasse.

10. Fan first half of basic, second half of basic turning to the left to lead lady forward in front and then turn lady ½ turn to be facing you in fan position.

11. The Alamena right foot back leading lady to make a three step turn in a triangular pattern while replacing weight to the left and doing a chase on the spot.

12. Hockey Stick forward check closing lady's feet, lead lady forward from fan position to cross in front and pass you lifting left hand to make a window as she goes by leading lady forward to a hockey stick like angle while locking behind her, then turn her to face you.

13. Hockey Stick Ending in Counter Promenade Position same as hockey stick ending in counter promenade.

14. Natural Top right foot behind left foot, then left foot to side and continue turning right. Try to make the shoulders rotate even more than the feet.

15. Natural Opening Out left foot forward opening partner out to the right, replace weight to the right foot bringing partner back to closed position, left foot chasse. Repeat on right side.

16. Closed Hip Twist left foot to side turning lady ½ turn right, replace weight to right foot turning partner back to the right ¾ turn. On your compact chasse bring partner across in front as she does a small forward step.

Silver Level International Cha Cha

17. Open Hip Twist Same as closed hip twist with more hip rotation for the lady.
18. Reverse Top right foot to side and slightly forward, swivel on the ball of the left foot ending left heal opposite right toe with toes turned out. Repeat.
19. Opening Out from Reverse Top from the reverse top, right foot to side and slightly forward turning left, left foot in front of right foot heel to toe with toe turned out turning left, right foot to side and slightly forward turning left, FR to side and slightly forward turning left, move left foot towards from of right foot toe turned out turning left, right foot to side and slightly forward turning left completing 3/8 left turn over the five steps.
20. Spiral left foot side, replace weight to right foot, left foot closes to right foot for LRL chase, right foot back, replace weight to left foot, right foot side chase while leading lady to do a spiral turn, which is a turn around the standing leg.
21. Curl left foot forward, replace weight to right foot, left foot to side to chasse LRL compact chasse, right foot back leading 5/8 turn left, replace weight to left foot, right to side and slightly forward RLR chasse completing ½ turn left over the last five steps.
22. Rope Spin Commence on the last step of the preceding figure, when man leads lady to turn sharply to her right under his raised left arm as he shapes to the right releasing hold with his right hand to end with lady on his right side facing the opposite direction. left foot to side leading spiral turn for lady, replace weight to right foot, left foot closes to right foot to chasse LRL to end in side-by-side position, right foot back, replace weight to left foot, right foot closes to left foot RLR chasse.
23. Aida commences in facing position, right foot back in Fallaway, left foot back in Fallaway, right foot back to chasse RLR locking action. Figure turns ¼ right over the five steps.
24. Cross Basic left foot forward in checking action turning ¼ turn left over the first five steps, right foot back, left foot to side and slightly forward to chasse LRL, right foot crosses behind left foot, left foot forward right foot to side and slightly back to chasse RLR turning ¼ left over the second five steps.
25. Cuban Breaks Count 2&3&4&1, left foot forward and across with 1/8 turn R, replace weight to right foot, left foot to side with 1/8 turn L, replace weight to right foot, left foot forward and across with 1/8 turn R, replace weight to right

foot, left foot to side with 1/8 turn L. Can switch and repeat on the other side. Maybe danced without the small turns or with ½ turns.

Cuban Break timing summary

1 side, 2 forward check, 2 ½ replace, 3 ¼ foot out flick through middle, 3 ¾ roll hip out and around, 4 check forward, 4

26. Chase' Open position without hold, left foot forward and turn (now lady is behind), close right foot to left foot without weight, forward lock RLR, left foot forward in line with right foot then turn to end left foot back with lady in front, forward lock LRL following lady, continue again. End by not turning.

Rumba

Sometimes called the "dance of love," Rumba is not a progressive dance; it is danced in an area of the floor. It is distinguished by its romantic feel and sensual hip action (Cuban Motion). The footwork is Ball Flat throughout. Toes should be slightly turned out. The feet or toes keep in contact with the floor using slight pressure.

Use the entire two beats of each "slow" count of music. Delay the settling of the hip until the end of the 2nd beat. Body movement should interpret the slow and romantic Rumba music. The rhythm used in Rumba is SQQ. At times the QQS may be a more appropriate way to think of the music. More advanced dancers can adjust the timing by using extra slows or by adding syncopations between the quicks.

Stand with a top forward position with weight on the front part of the foot to create connection with partner. Maintain same height throughout the dance, keeping the head level and shoulders relaxed. Do not tilt the shoulders from side to side.

Use correct Cuban Motion, being sure to step with the knee flexed and delay straightening. Keep ribcage lifted and moving in opposition to the hips. Take small steps. Lead and follow from the center of the body, using compression and leverage. Use the free arm in a natural way from the body to express the music and complement the body movement.

American Rumba Bronze

1. Side Basic Side, together, side, left or right. SQQ is the normal rhythm but it can be QQS.
2. Fifth Position Side, other foot behind (5th position), replace weight, left or right. The figure can be done in hand-to-hand position or arm on back position.
3. Box Step 1st half: left foot forward S, right foot side Q, left foot close changing weight Q, 2nd half: right foot back, left foot side, right foot close. Figure can be done straight or with up to a 1/4 rotation to the left.
4. Cross body Lead Start with 1st half a box, then right foot back stepping off the track turning left ¼ turn while leading partner walk two steps forward on SQ, left foot side, right foot closes to left foot leading partner to third step forward, then a sharp turn to the left to face leader. This is SQQ timing.
Alternatively use QQS timing, start with a side step to the right on S, break forward and replace on QQ, then a ¼ turn to the left and step left on S leading partner walk forward on S, rock back on Q and replace on second Q and turn ¼ turn to the left while leading partner to turn ½ turn left, step right on S.

5. Outside Partner Start with a Cross Body Lead, then left foot side, right foot forward and left-to-right outside partner leading partner to step back, replace weight to left foot, right foot side left foot forward and right to left outside position leading partner to step back, replace weight to right foot. End by adding 2nd half of a box or an under-arm turn.

6. Slow Underarm Turn 1st half of box, 2nd half of box rotating to the left leading partner forward and off to the left for two Measure walk around turn, 1st half of box while partner completes walk around turn, 2nd half of box collecting partner.

7. Open Break Underarm Turn 1st half of box, open break (right foot side, left foot back leading partner to rock back as well, replace weight to right foot), right foot 5th position break (left foot side, right foot behind left foot leading under arm turn right {spot turn for follower}, replace weigh to left foot), side basic to right.

8. Crossover Break 1st half of box, left foot crossover break (right foot side right arm preparing for turn, ¼ turn to right checking with left foot, replace weight to right foot), right foot crossover, left foot crossover, side basic to right or another figure to end. Crossover breaks can be done in a variety of combinations.

9. Crossover & Side Rocks 1st half of box, left foot crossover break, right foot side rock (after replacing weight to the right foot in the crossover, replace weight to the left foot which you have left in place S for the extra rocking action, ¼ turn to the left and right foot side Q, replace weight to the left foot Q), another left foot crossover break, another right foot side rock, finish with the 2nd half of a box.

10 Open Rumba Walks Cross body lead to open out on leader's left side, left foot forward, right foot side, replace weight to left foot, 3 back walks in left side partner, 3 back walks in open facing position, 2nd half of box.

11. Shoulder Check 1st half of box, open break, shoulder check (left foot side, right foot forward and across, replace weight to left foot leading follower's inside under arm turn left, lower left hand to stop turn and place right hand on follower's shoulder blade to stop turn), lead partner back out with an outside under arm turn right, repeat in, repeat out, right foot 5th position break leading follower to under arm turn right, side basic to right.

12. Cradle Circle 1st half of box, open break into Double hand hold, leading partner to turn into cradle position and do 3 forward walks while partner does 3 back walks, right foot forward, left foot side break in Right Cradle Position, close then two forward walks while partner does slow under arm turn right to roll out of cradle, side basic to right.

13. Quick Underarm Turn & Loop 1st half of box, right foot back, left foot side break while follower does quick under arm turn right, left foot forward check in fan position while follower does quick under arm turn left, replace weight to right foot side then left foot forward break, left foot side to right foot 5th position break while follower does a spot under arm turn right, side break to right to finish.

14. Open Circular Walks 1st half of box, right foot back then left foot side break, while follower begins a slow under arm turn right, ending in open hammer lock position, OHLP, replace weight to left foot while follower completes turn then two forward walks in OHLP, three forward walks in OHLP, to exit OHLP, left foot forward, right foot forward check with follower under arm turn left, right foot side to left foot crossover break, left foot side to right foot 5th position break while follower does spot under arm turn right, ending with a side basic to the right.

15. Spot Turn Combination 1st half of a box while follower does a under arm turn left, right foot side to open break, three Measures of back spot turns, right foot close to left foot side break (an opening out), two Measures of forward spot turn, left foot side to right foot forward break in right outside partner, 2nd half of box to finish. Spot turns are done in closed position. The back spot-turn starts with a left foot side step, blocking partner, followed by a hook step (placement of the right foot behind the left foot in this case), then another side step in rotation. The top of the frame should be leading the turn to the right. The rotation over three Measures can be up to 2 complete turns. Hook step, side step is repeated for the three Measures (or one Measure for a shorter spot turn). The book figure includes the forward spot turn, but either the back or forward spot turns can be done by themselves.

To increase the difficulty of the figures, note that any time partner is moving to the side, an under-arm turn can be led in the direction of that movement. Adding rotation to the figures may give them a different look.

Rumba Bronze Variations

1. Butterfly (Cha Cha) Crossover break followed by a 5th position break side-by-side.

2. Check and Circular Walk (Bolero) A forward check, followed by an inside under arm turn to a forward natural top for two Measures with a side-by-side back break to end.

3. Romantic Sways (Bolero) Same as Bolero figure 7.

4. Hip Twist and Spin (Bolero) Same as Bolero figure 10.

5. Side Breaks (Mambo figure 2) Side replace close.

6. Crossover Break and Walk Around Turn (Mambo figure 6) Three crossover breaks alternating sides with a both turn free spins on the fourth Measures.

7. Alternating Underarm Turns (Mambo figure 9) Quick underarm turns for follower on both sides. A man's turn could be added.

8. Cross Body Lead with Inside Turn (Mambo) An inside under arm turn is added and the end of the cross-body lead while moving side to the right. An inside turn can be added almost any time partner is moving to the side.

9. Back Spot Turn (Mambo) Starts with an open break, three Measures and then 5th position break to end.

10. Extended Box (Samba) Rumba box with four quick side steps added at each of the box.

11. Shadow positions (Cha Cha figure 10) From right-to-right hand hold, a cross body lead to end in left side shadow position over 3 Measures. Starts with a side step to the right on slow, a forward break on Q, replace on Q turning left ¼ turn, lead partner to left side in shadow while rocking back and replace on the 23, S to the right, left foot crossover break in left shadow position on Q, replace on Q, repeat with 2nd half of cross body lead ending in left shadow position , left foot cross over break in left shadow position then turn ¼ left and side step L, end with under arm turn right for partner.

12. Crab Walks start in promenade position with inside foot moving forward, turn to face partner and take a side step, turn back to promenade position then inside foot moves forward.

13. Pivots start in promenade position, rotate 180 around the right leg blocking partner, continues turns to the right with right inside thy to right inside thy of partner take with the rotation. See promenade pivots in Waltz.

American Rumba Silver

1. Alternating Underarm Turns Open break, side basic to the left in open facing partner position with follower doing a under arm turn right, follower does a side basic back in open facing partner position while leader does a under arm turn right, side basic to left in open facing partner position follower does under arm turn right, grapevine to the right in closed position, grapevine to the right and side rock closed position to outside facing partner position to promenade position, syncopated &SQQ promenade run in promenade position and side basic in open facing partner position to left while follower does under arm turn right, side basic to right in open facing partner position.

2. Open Swivel Walks 1st half of box, cross body lead, side rock to right, back walks turning right, side step to back walks turning left, side step to back walks turning right, side basic to left while follower does under arm turn right, 5th position break ending in closed position.

3. Left Side Catch, Cradle & Roll Out Cross over break, side basic to left with follower under arm turn right, side step with under arm turn left and back rock, under arm turn with side basic to left while follower rolls in to right arm, side step to right and left foot back rock while follower does a under arm turn right, 1st half of box, 2nd half of box.

4. Quick Underarm Turn 1st half of box, back step with side rock to left while follower does under arm turn left, open break, side step and back rock with follower's under arm turn right and cross body lead, forward walks.

5. Roll Out, Circle Wrap Open break, back spot turn to right changing hands behind follower's back while follower dances pivot turns to the right, open break, man turns to left and dances into lady's right arm then dances two steps of grapevine right while lady pivots right into man's right arm, in right side shadow position, forward walk into right foot check then replace and close while lady checks back and then pivots to her left.

6. Spiral Swivel 1st half of box, left foot side break while lady does 5th position break, right foot side break while lady dances spiral to swivel to her left, right foot forward outside partner turning to right then left foot side break while lady dances 5th position break, FR side break while lady dances spiral to swivel to her left, right foot forward OP turning to right then left foot side break while lady dances 5th position break, right foot side break while lady dances 5th position break, left foot side break as lady dances 5th position break.

7. Shadow Variations Open break, grapevine moving left and turning right while lady does a spot under arm turn right, forward walk to left foot forward check while lady walks and checks back on right foot, right foot side rock while lady does spot under arm turn right, forward walk to left foot forward check while lady walks and checks back on right foot, right foot side rock while lady does spot

Clarke Fairbrother – Dance Nuggets

under arm turn right, forward walks turning right while lady walks back release all hold and regain closed hold on last Q, left foot side step and promenade walks while lady swivels to her right and walks in promenade, left foot side rock.

8. Swivel Combination Open break, left foot to side then stationary rocks while lady steps forward and swivels under man's raised left arm to left then swivels to right and left in TP, continue stationary rocks and swivels, one stationary rock and cross body lead to end in closed position while lady swivels and walks forward and then back turning left, right foot side step then check across in opposition break while lady dances right foot side break, left foot to side then stationary rocks while lady steps forward and swivels to right and then left then right, continue stationary rocks while lady continues to swivel, one stationary rock and a cross body lead while lady swivels right and then cross body lead, right foot side break.

9. Open Rumba Walks & Swivels right foot side break with turn to right while lady does spot under arm turn left, three back walks turning right while lady walks back, side step turning lady to face then forward and side while lady does double spot under arm turn left, three back walks turning right while lady walks back, side step turning lady to face then forward and side while lady does double spot under arm turn left, side step turning lady to face then back walks while lady forward walks, 2nd half to box to finish.

10. Man's Wrap Open break, syncopated &SQQ close to side rocks while lady does quick under arm turn to side rocks, side rock to cross body lead, right foot side step to man's under arm turn while lady dances back break, two back walks and left foot forward pivot, open break with double hand hold.

International Rumba Bronze

International Style Rumba uses the timing "2 3 4 (1)" where the 1 has no foot movement, only body movement. The movement is similar to American Rumba; however, the styling is to arrive on a straight leg instead of the bent leg.

1. Basic Movement left foot back, replace weight to right foot, left foot forward then right foot forward, replace weight to left foot, right foot back.
2. Alternative Basic Close left foot to right foot with pressure but without weight; replace weight to right foot, left foot to side. The figure is also danced the other way, by starting with closing right foot to left foot.
3. Cucarachas While standing on two straight legs with feet flat on the floor, rotate the hips with a Cuban, figure 8, action.
4. New Yorker is the same as crossover breaks in American. left foot crossover break (right foot side right arm preparing for turn, ¼ turn to right checking with left foot, replace weight to right foot), right foot crossover, left foot crossover, side basic to right or another figure to end.
5. Spot Turns Spot turns for both partners on the 2 3 and a side step on the 41.
6. Shoulder to Shoulder is the same as Outside Partner in American. left foot side, right foot forward and left-to-right outside partner leading partner to step back, replace weight to left foot, right foot side left foot forward and right to left outside partner position, leading partner to step back, replace weight to right foot.
7. Hand-to-hand Similar to a 5th position break in American. Here the partners are in hand-to-hand position as they alternate sides of hand-to-hand position instead of wing position.
8. Progressive Walks Forward & Back The walks can be done facing partner or side-by-side with partner. Forward walks are normal commenced on the left foot and back walks on the right foot. Walks are normally done in groups of 3 or 6 steps.
9. Side Steps closed position, left foot side, right foot closes to left foot, left foot side, right foot closes to left foot, left foot side, right foot closes to left foot.
10. Cuban Rocks Fall away Position, feet apart weight on right foot, use Cuban motion to move the hip weight from foot to foot with the legs straight. Also call cucarachas.
11. The Fan closed position, 1st half of a basic, right foot back leading partner forward and across in front of leader, replace weight to left foot beginning to turn partner to the left, right foot side leading partner back and completing her turn so that she is in fan or OFP to leader's left.
12. The Alamena from fan or OPF, a three step under arm turn right for follower taking all forward steps in a triangular pattern turning at each corner of the triangle. From the fan the leader steps left foot forward (closing partner's feet),

replace, left foot closes to right foot, right foot back leading the turn, replace leading the turn, right foot closes to left foot finishing the turn.

13. Hockey Stick from fan position, leader steps left foot forward (closing partner's feet), replace, left foot closes to right foot, right foot back leading partner forward with a hand raised to look through the window, replace left foot leading partner to turn ½ turn left and now that she is facing you to step back, right foot forward leading partner to step back.

14. The Hockey Stick Ending in Counter Promenade position from fan, left foot forward closing lady, replace to right foot leading lady forward, left foot closes to right foot leading lady forward raising arm, right foot diagonally back turning to right while leading lady to turn left, replace to left foot continuing to turn lady and bring arm down, right foot diagonally forward continuing to turn lady's 7/8 turn ending in closed position.

15. Natural Top closed position, right foot behind left foot toe to heel commence right turn, left foot to side, repeat three more times while completing up to 2 full turns, end on the ninth step closing right foot to left foot. Legs should be flexed when the feet are crossed and straighten when the feet are apart. The turn should be continuous remaining square with partner, leading the turn with the right side. Tops do not have much hip movement.

16. Opening Out to Right and Left closed position, left foot side releasing partner's right hand and moving her to right side position, replace weight to right foot, left foot closes to right foot shaping to left bringing partner to left side, right foot side moving partner to left side position, replace weight to left foot bringing partner to closed position, right foot closes to left foot ending closed position.

17. Natural Opening Out closed position, left foot side leading partner to right, replace to right foot leading partner back to closed position, left foot closes to right foot ending in closed position.

18. Closed Hip Twist closed position, left foot side opening partner out ½ turn to right, replace, left foot closes to right foot while partner completes ½ turn left, right foot back while partner turns 3/8 turn to right, replace while partner continues up to ½ turn left, right foot diagonally forward leading partner to finish turn ending in fan position.

International Rumba Silver Level

19) Open Hip Twist from open facing position, left foot forward closing lady's feet, replace weight to right foot leading lady forward , left foot closes to right foot leading lady forward, right foot back lead lady to twist tor her right, replace weight to left foot leading lady to twist right, right foot side end in fan position lead lady to ½ left turn and step back.

20) Reverse Top from closed facing position, right foot to side and slightly forward, swivel on the ball of left foot turning to left, right foot side and slightly forward, repeat swivel on ball of left foot and right foot side and slightly forward three times. Left side leads in left turning figure. Lead the rotation from the top. No hip action in tops.

21) Opening Out from Reverse Top from closed facing position as from preceding figure, right foot side and slightly forward turning left leading lady to fan position by releasing right hand and holding left hand in normal position as body turns, left foot in front of right foot continue left turn turning lady ½ turn more, right foot side and slightly forward leading lady back into in fan position.

22) Aida from closed facing position after 6 steps of reverse top, three back walks turning right ending in V-shaped position.

23) Spiral left foot to side with slight right turn leading lady to turn up to ½ turn right, replace weight to right foot commence turning left leading lady to turn ½ turn left, right foot back, replace weight to left foot commence turning left leading lady to turn ½ turn left over these two steps, right foot to side and slightly forward continuing to turn ¼ left during the last two steps.

24) Curl Commence in open facing position left hand to right hand hold, left foot forward replace weight to right foot, left foot closes to right foot leading lady to turn left, right foot back lady turns ¾ turn left, replace weight to left foot lady continuing to turn left, right foot to side lady continuing to turn ½ turn left.

25) Rope Spin Commence on the last step of the preceding figure, when man leads lady to turn sharply to her right under his raised left arm as he shapes to the right releasing hold with his right hand to end with lady on his right side facing the opposite direction. left foot to side leading spiral turn for lady, replace weight to right foot, left foot closes to right foot to end in side-by-side position, right foot back, replace weight to left foot, right foot closes to left foot. Lady completes a rope spin on first step of figure and walks around man for the balance of the six steps.

East Coast Swing

East Coast Swing is an, upbeat, non-progressive dance. The basic step for swing is rock step, triple step to the left and triple step to the right. Swing has bounce, a back break (also called a "rock step"), and "swing hip action". The basic count is 1 2, 3a4, 5a6 (The "a" count is equal to 1/4 of a beat of music. Swing timing is 1 2 3a4 5a6 however extended figures use 12 3a4 56 7a8.

The closed position in swing is a dance position where the Leader's right side and Follower's left side are almost in contact and the opposite sides are open in a very slight V- shape. The Leader's left hand is held at Follower's waist level in a cup position, and the Follower's right-hand hooks lightly over the Leader's hand. The Leader's right hand is placed on the Follower's left shoulder blade, and the Follower's left-hand rests on the Leader's right shoulder. The Follower should be slightly offset to the Leader's right. Stand with the weight on the forward part of the foot (weight forward) to create connection with partner. Many figures in swing are danced in two hand hold or handshake hold to facilitate under arm turns and spins.

The rock step for both partners is a small step back for each partner on the 1 replacing the weight and moving the pelvis forward on the 2. Rock Steps are danced ball flat, ball flat (BF, BF), or ball, ball flat (B, BF). Try to keep the upper body and head forward while taking the back step.

Side triples (side, close, side) may be danced BF, BF, B facing partner or for slow music BF, B, BF. Most common footwork is B, BF, BF. Keep the weight forward on all "rock steps" (back breaks). Take small steps. Lead and follow from the center of the body, using compression and tension. Use the free arm in a natural way to complement the music and body movement. Toes should be slightly turned out throughout. Keep feet or toes in contact with the floor.

The starting body position for a triple step is to settle into the right hip while the rib cage moves to the left. Lift the left foot so the toe is dragging on the floor and take a very small step left to the ball of the left foot. While holding the right hip to the right, bring the right foot into the left first on the ball of the foot then ball flat. With the right hip still to the right, push off the right foot for a regular sized step to the left. Slide the left toe across the floor while making the step. After full weight is on left foot, swing the hips all the way over to the left with the left hip a bit forward and the rib cage to the right. The right knee should now be bent with the toe barely touching the floor or even raised in the air like Jive. Now you are ready to triple back to the right using the same technique.

East Coast Swing uses "swing" hip action" and bounce. The bounce is created by flexing and straightening the knees with knees relaxed throughout. Normal Cuban Motion is used on rock steps (back breaks) and "swing hip action" on all triple steps. On triple steps, the "swing hip action" is different from Rumba in that the hips do not change on every step, during a triple step, the dancer delays swinging and settling the hip to the new side until the end of the third step of the triple.

Side triple step travels sideways, either to the right or left, side, close, side.

A forward triple step travels forward, where the second step does not pass the first step, and the third step continues moving forward. The foot position for the second step is: instep of second step to the heel of the first step.

A forward running triple travels forward, where the feet pass each other on each step. This is danced by the Follower on counts 3 a4 of a throw-out, and on counts 3 a4 of the Whirlpool.

In a delayed forward triple step, the first two steps are danced in place, and the third step advances forward.

A back-triple step travels backward where the second step does not pass the first step, and the third step continues moving backward. The foot position for the second step is: heel of second step to the instep of the first step.

A triple in place is a step where all three steps are danced in place.

A Turning triple is a step in which significant turn is made. This is danced by the Follower in Tuck-Ins, Alternating Underarm Turns, and the Opposition and Roll Out.

East Coast Swing Bronze
1. Basic Starts in swing closed position left foot back with 1/8 turn to left leading partner to rock back in Fallaway position, replace weight to right foot returning to Swing closed position. These two steps are the rock step. This is followed by a left foot side triple step and then a right foot side triple step.
2. Basic turning to the Right This figure is a basic with each of the triple steps turning ¼ turn to the right.
3. Basic turning to the Left This figure is a basic with each of the triple steps turning ¼ turn to the left.

4. Throw out Rock step, ¼ turn left then a forward triple with small steps pulling partner is to do a forward running triple across leader's body with larger steps and turn ½ getting to facing position, then right foot side triple.

5. Underarm Turn (inside turn) From facing position lead an open break (like the rock step with little rotation), left foot side triple leading follower's under arm turn left at the end of the triple, after completion of the under-arm turn, right foot side triple in Facing position. This step can be repeated.

6. Underarm Release from Basic First the under-arm turn out: From facing position lead an rock step, left foot side triple. Then lead follower's 180 under arm turn right (an outside turn) at the end of the triple, after completion of the under arm turn lead partner to triple to her left while leader triples to the right.

Second the underarm turn in: This is a under arm turn left back to swing closed position or facing position. It starts with an open break, then a left foot side triple towards partner as follower triples toward leader. Lead a follower's inside under arm turn left at the end of the triple then right foot side triple. This can end in either swing closed position or facing position. Leader makes a ¼ turn to the right at the beginning of the second triple.

This figure is a combination of two underarm turn figures that can be danced separately.

7. Tuck - Ins (referred to as an American Spin in Jive) A) Handshake B) Right to Left C) Double Hand From any of the hand holds start with and open break then triple in place or slightly forward with a right-side lead to give compression in the connection to partner, just before 5 (the beginning of the 2nd triple led partner to spin one turn to the right, finish with a right foot triple in place or a triple to the right after partner spins. End in left-to-right hand hold. The turn for the follower is normally a free spin, but it can be a under arm turn.

8. Alternating Underarm Turns Start with an underarm release from basic, then an open break followed by a left foot side turning right while follower does a under arm turn left, then leaders under arm turn left.

9. Shoulder Check Shoulder Check is an 8-count pattern 12 3a4 56 7a8. Open break on 12, ¼ turn right and left foot side triple with an under arm turn left on 3a4 leader catching turning partner's back to limit turn to ½ turn (at this point partner will know it is a shoulder check, not an under-arm turn), right foot forward break still holding partner's left shoulder (the shoulder check) 56, right foot side triple turning left ¼ turn with under arm turn right to facing position 7a8. This figure is commonly done in sets of two.

10. Cradle Open break in Double hand hold, left foot forward triple while leading a under arm turn left with your left hand and continuing to hold partner's left hand with your right hand ending in right cradle position, right foot triple back in right cradle position (the roll in), left foot break back (the rock step) in right cradle position, left foot forward triple from right cradle position with Funder arm turn right (the roll out), right foot side triple completing under arm turn right to facing position in Double hand hold. This is a two six count pattern.

11. Cradle to Hammer Lock Start with the Cradle above, then reverse the turns to make it a hammer lock instead of a cradle. The hammer lock can be done without the cradle from Double hand hold position.

12. Sugar Push Throw Out First the Sugar Push: open break in Double hand hold, left foot forward triple with 1/8 turn left to bring partner to Sugar Push position (leader's right side to follower's right side), right foot side triple with a sharp 3/8 turn right at the end of the 4 beat.

Second the throw out: open break in Double hand hold, left foot triple in place while raising the right arm and lowering the left arm to lead follower to do a forward running triple, right foot side triple in facing position. The first and second parts may be danced as separate parts and either portion can be danced two or more times consecutively.

13. Double Face Loop First the under arm turn and face loops: Open break in cross hand hold with left hand on top, left foot side triple turning right with follower under arm turn left maintaining hold of both hands (after the under arm turn the right hand will be on top), right foot side triple with two face loops (both over the leader's head) ending in swing closed position.

Second the sharp turning rotating basic to the left: Rock step back and side turning 1/4 to the left in right angle position, right foot forward running triple with very small steps for leader while leading follower to run around with ½ turn to left in right angle position ending Swing closed position, ¼ turn left and right foot side triple in Swing closed position. The modified rock step is used to start the turning action and create momentum.

14. Opposition Break & Roll Out From right opening out position (similar to the right angle position) do an opening out or opposition break which is break to the left and replace while leading partner to go back and come forward, left foot compact forward triple leading follower to a under arm turn left leader turning ¼ turn left on beat 4, forward right side triple in facing position.

15. Whirlpool All in Swing closed position rotating 1½ turns to the right through the figure. 12 two forward walks turning right, 3a4 left foot side triple turning right while follower does a forward triple, 5a6 back side forward (a grapevine) turning right while follower does a side triple. Figure can be repeated. This is similar to a natural top in other dances.

16. Helicopter or Back Taps (not in Divida American Syllabus, called Chugging in Jive Gold) Lead and American spin but keep right-to-right hand hold for a series of hip twists. Rock step with ¼ turn to the right on 2, ¼ turn to the right and right foot triple touching partners shoulder with the right hand, ¾ turn to the right and left foot triple partner touching your shoulder, ¼ turn to the

Clarke Fairbrother – Dance Nuggets

right and right foot triple touching partner's shoulder, ¾ turn to the right and left foot triple partner touching your shoulder.

17. Back Walks, Kicks and Flicks, from facing positions back rock into fallaway position, then take three more walks back, point step with outside legs, point step with inside legs, then turn to face partner, and do point step towards partner and repeat with the other leg, then normal rock step and back to basic.

East Coast Swing Silver

1. Wrist Spin & Alternating Turn Open break, forward triple taking lady's right wrist with right hand, side triple turning left while partner does a solo turn to the right, repeat, open break, side triple to right (lady under arm turn to left), side triple turning left turning left under own arm while lady does a triple left.

2. Face Loops & Tuck Spin Open break in cross double hand hold left over right, side triple left with lady under arm turn left, side triple right with right then left-hand loops. Fallaway break, tuck in, side triple right, with lady double under arm turn right.

3. Tuck In, Alternating Hammerlock Open break and side triple to tuck in position, side triple to right with lady under arm turn right ending in lady's hammerlock, back break, side triple with lady's under arm turn left to man's hammer lock lady triples in place, back break turning triple to left with lady under arm turn left, side triple right.

4. Two Hand Catch & Spin Open break, triple in place with lady forward triple curving right end in tandem position, triple in place, forward break with lady back break, triple in place with lady forward triple curving right, side triple right lady under arm turn R, Fallaway break, side triple left, side triple right with lady under arm turn right.

5. Rotating Basic Open break, side triple with lady under arm turn L, hook triple turning right, 2 forward walks, side triple left turning right, forward triple turning right, 2 forward walks, side triple left turning right, forward triple turning right, side break with lady back break, triple in place turning left with lady running triple, side triple right.

6. Side to Side & Running Pass or Sliding Doors. Open break, side triple left with lady triple right in front of man ending on man's right side, back break, side triple to right with lady solo turn to right behind man end in outside facing position. Repeat.

7. Boogie Walks Open break, side triple left with lady under arm turn left, hook triple with right foot tap ending to change feet while lady does a forward triple turning right-to-right side partner. Now both have weight on left foot. Boogie walks 12, 34, 56, 7 count taking turns stepping in front of each other. End with a triple in place then a side triple right with double under arm turn right for lady.

8. Rhythm Variations A) Pull Back, B) Sailor Shuffle or hook triples, hook behind, step out the same direction as the hook, then step back the other direction with a bit of falling motion.

9. Twist & Face or Trading Places turn starts one hand hold with a rock back open break, turn ¼ to the right leading partner forward while tripling to the left, raising hand to look at partner "through the window" as she passes like in a hockey stick. At the end of the triple turn ¼ to the right leading partner to a ½ turn to her left, finish with a triple to the right.

10. Wrap Combination Open break, forward triple close right-to-right, side triple to right, forward break with lady back break, tuck in, side triple to right with lady double under arm turn right, back break, side triple with lady double under arm turn left, turning triple in place with lady back triple, forward break with lady back break, turning triple in place with lady forward triple, side triple with lady double under arm turn right.

11. Progressive closed series w kickball changes (not Syllabus) starts in closed position with a fallaway rock step to promenade position on 1 2, then a forward lock triple in promenade position, then two kickball changes, then a forward lock triple in PP, forward step twisting to face partner, small side step twisting to PP in a lowered position, forward step twisting to face partner, small side step twisting to PP in a lowered position,

12. Chasse' turns in offset closed hold, triple right turning right, triple to the left turning right, triple right turning right, triple left turning right, like the Scatter Chasse in Quick step. **Partner on the inside of turn provides the power** for the turn.

13. Hook Whips start with a basic rock step and triple step. Leader then hooks his right foot behind his left leading partner to rotate to the right as in a natural top. Left foot then moves to the side and forward to continue the rotation. This can be done one or more times. Exit from the whip (top) with a triple to the right. This figure should be done on a wide expanded frame.

14. Pivot Whips start with a basic rock step and triple step. On the third step of the triple the leader steps back with an Ugly Foot to begin the rotation. Leader then rotates 180 around the right leg blocking partner, and continues the rotation as in pivots above. This figure should be done in a close closed frame with inner thigh to inner thigh connection as in a waltz or foxtrot pivot. **Partner on the inside of turn provides the power**. Exit from the whip (pivot) with a triple to the right.

Jive Bronze

Jive is very similar to swing, danced to faster music. Jive is danced more straight up than swing with smaller steps and a bit of bounce.

1. Basic in Place Rock step, triple to the left, triple to the right.
2. Fallaway Rock, Rock step, triple to the left, triple to the right with bigger steps.
3. Fallaway Throwaway Rock step, triple to the left releasing partner, triple to the right with partner is single had hold.
4A. Link Rock Just like basic
4B. Link A basic that starts in single hand hold, and ends in closed position.
5. Change of Places Right to Left Starts in closed with an inside under arm turn to single hand hold.
6. Change of Places Left-to-right Starts in single hand hold (as figure 5 ended) with an inside under arm turn to single hand hold on the other side.
7. Change of Hands behind the Back from single hand hold, triple towards partner, changing to right-to-right hand hold then turning to exchange hands behind the back to left-to-right hand hold.
8. Hip Bump From single hand hold, rock step, lead partner to be on your left side by extending the left hand forward, then triple to the side towards partner bumping hips at the end of the triple, ends with a triple away from partner.
9. American Spin Starts in right-to-right hand hold, rock step, then a forward triple building compression in the connection, leading partner to spin at the end of the first triple. While partner turns on the second triple, triple in place.
10. The Walks Starts in closed position, rock step, a left side triple, turn ¼ turn to the left with partner turning a ¼ turn to the right for a forward triple.
11. Stop & Go Same as a shoulder check in swing. 12 rock step, 3a4 lead partner for an inside turn as you turn ¼ to the right and place right hand on partner's shoulder to stop her turn, 56 check forward in front of partner while she checks back, 7&8 lead partner's outside turn back out while you turn ¼ left back to original position.
12. The Mooch Kicks and flicks in right side-by-side hands on each other's shoulders position.
13. The Whip Hook behind turning left ¼ turn and replace for 12, triple to the left for 3&4 end in closed position.
14. The Whip Throwaway Hook behind turning left ¼ turn and replace for 12, triple to the left for 3&4 end in open position.

Jive Silver

15. Reverse Whip Starting in closed position, rock step, then a triple, 56 going forward turning right, 7&8 triple turning right.
16. Windmill A turning basic with arms spread on 3&4.
17. Spanish Arms Roll almost into cradle and then reverse back out on 5&6.
18. Rolling Off the Arm Roll into cradle on 3&4, walk around in cradle 56, roll out of cradle with right arm on 7&8,
19. Simple Spin Turn a ¼ turn, step forward, spin 1 turn either direction.
20. Miami Special Starts in handshake or right-to-right hand hold, rock step then under arm turn right partner to your left side putting partner's arm over your head then triple away with arm slide to regain left-to-right hand hold. Add a hip bump when partner is at your left side if you want.
21. Overturned Fallaway Throwaway Starts with a fallaway throwaway overturning partner at the end of the throwaway so that she is facing away from you, then turn her to face you.

Jive Gold

22) Point, Ball Change 1a2 left foot point, left foot behind right foot, replace weight to right foot, 3a4 left foot triple to the side, 5a6 right foot point, right foot behind left foot, replace weight to left foot, 7a8 right foot triple to the side.
23) Curly Whip 12 left foot forward, replace weight to right foot while turning ½ turn to right, 3a4 left foot side chase turning right ¼ turn.
24) Shoulder Spin Same as American cradle with leader's right hand to follower's shoulder leading follower's spin to right on the way out of the cradle.
25) Toe Heel Swivels 123456 left foot point toe down, left foot point heel down, left foot cross in front of right foot, right foot point toe down, right foot point heel down, right foot cross in front of left foot.
26) Chugging Same as Helicopter in Bronze Swing.
27) Chicken Walks 12345678 leader walks backwards leading follower to swivel on each step, 12 3a4 5a6 throw-out with overturn ending. The figure can now be repeated going the other way.
28) Catapult 12 rock step in right-to-right hand hold, 3a4 partner is lead down leader's left side and under arm turned ½ turn right to be facing the same direction as partner while leader is doing triple in place, 5a6 triple in place while giving other hand to partner who is now behind the leader, 12 forward rock while partner back rocks, 3a4 partner now triple forward on leaders left side while leader triples in place, 5a6 triple in place giving partner a spin to the right with the left hand to come back to left-to-right Facing position.

29) Stalking Walks, Flicks and Break 12 left foot rock back and replace, 3 left foot point forward, 4 left foot step, 5 right foot point forward, 6 right foot step, 7 left foot point forward, 8 close, 1 right foot flick, 2 step closed, 3 flick, 4 close, 5 flick, 6 close, 7 flick, 8 close, 1 step forward, 23 hold, 4& left foot forward ball right foot change.

30) Overturned Change of Places Left-to-right First figure: 123a45a6 Change of places with a double turn on the 5a6 with leader putting right hand on partner's left shoulder to lead double turn.

Second figure: 12 rock step, prepare for turn on 2, 3a4 triple in place with partner does an inside double under arm turn L, 5a 6 triple to the right.

Bolero

Bolero is a romantic dance characterized by slow, smooth, gliding movements, graceful turns, and dramatic arm styling. Bolero uses contra body movement from Tango, rise and fall from Waltz, and a modified version of Cuban motion from Rumba. Bolero is danced to slow Latin music.

Using Foot Rise (at the end of each slow count), the rise may be taken all the way to the toe, much like the rise used in Waltz. Toes should be slightly turned out throughout. Keep feet in contact with the floor.

"Drop and Drift" action is used on all forward and back breaks. "Drop and Drift" allows the dancer an opportunity to feature beautiful leg lines dropping (lowering) on the first step of a forward or back break (1st Quick), and drifting (travelling and reaching) on the second step of a forward or back break (2nd Quick). The drifting, or reaching leg, is fully extended with slight turnout and toes pointed. The "drops" are achieved by taking a small step under the body, and the "drifts" are accomplished by taking a larger, reaching step.

The Bolero frame is a blend of a Ballroom and a Latin frame. The frame is wider than in the other Rhythm dances and the distance between partners is less, ranging from a few inches apart (as a beginner), to light body contact (for more advanced dancers).

Because Bolero is the slowest of all the Rhythm dances, there is an opportunity to emphasize and stretch all movements to their fullest capacity. Be sure to fill out all "Slows" for their full 2 beats of music. Bolero emphasizes the expressiveness of the free arm. The arms move in a balletic way with elongated sensual lines and expressive hands. Maintain good posture, keeping the head up and shoulders relaxed. Lead and follow from the center of the body, using compression and tension. Use the free arm to complement the music.

Bolero is danced SQQ.

Bolero Bronze Figures

1. Basic Movement closed position, left foot side, right foot back small step (drop), left foot forward (drift) for 1st half, right foot side, left foot back small step (drop), right foot forward (drift) for 2nd half of basic. The basic movement commonly turns to the left ¼ turn per Measure with most of the turn coming on the small step back (the drop) like a slip pivot.

2. Open Break and Underarm Turn first half of turning basic, forward break (open break) in OFP, left foot side, right foot 5th position break (follower spot under arm turn right), second half of turning basic.

3. Underarm Pass first half of basic, forward break ending offset right partner position, left foot closes, right foot back break (follower's under arm turn left), second half of basic. This is like a right-side pass with under arm turn.

4. Left Side Pass 1st half of basic, open break ending Offset LP, left foot side, right foot back break turning left, 2nd half of basic. This could be called a cross body lead.

5. Crossover Break 1st half of basic, right foot side and left foot cross over break, return to facing position LR side and raise right hand for simultaneous UA spot turns (leader left, follower right), 2nd half of basic.

6. Check and Circular Walk 1st half of basic, right foot side left foot forward check in fan position (follower right foot back break), side hook side to right outside partner (follower's underarm pass), capture follower into closed position for three circular walks in right outside partner, 1st half of basic with wind up and left turn, 2nd half of basic.

7. Romantic Sways closed position, three side rocks left right left, right foot side left foot crossover break, left foot forward in left side partner and two side rocks in double hand hold, right foot side left foot crossover break, left foot forward swivel to right foot forward check in open promenade position, right foot side left foot forward break (follower's spot under arm turn left), left foot side, spot under arm turn left (follower's back break), 2nd half of basic.

8. Check Underarm Pass 1st half of basic, forward open break, left foot side hook side (follower's checked underarm pass), right foot forward swivel and ronde turning to face partner left foot forward break, left foot close (follower's hip twist) right foot back turning basic, 2nd half of basic.

9. Spot Turn Combination 1st half of basic, forward open break, back spot turn (side, behind, side), back spot turn (behind, side behind) (follower's swivel and forward spot turn), complete spot turn (right foot side) second half of basic with contra check action and left turn, 1st half of basic with wind up and left turn, 2nd half of basic.

10. Hip Twist and Spin 1st half of basic, open break, left foot side (follower's hip twist) right foot turning back break, right foot side left foot crossover break, left foot side right foot 5th position break (follower's double spot under arm turn right SQ&Q&), right foot side left foot back break in RSP with follower's face loop, 1st half of basic with wind up and left turn, 2nd half of basic.

Bronze Bolero Variations
1 Outside Partner with Arm Loop
2 Hip Twist

3 She Turns, He Turns, She Turns with Variations
4 Curl to Rocks
5 Shadow with Alternative Around
6 Man's Walk Around
7 Aida to Rock
8 Man's Lunge to Pose
9 Crossover to Continuous Turns
10 Half left foot Basic to Ronde with Spot Turn
11 Fifth Position Breaks (Rumba)
12 Butterfly (Cha Cha)
13 Shoulder Check (Mambo)
14 Alternating Underarm Turns (Mambo)
15 Cross Body Lead with Inside Turn (Mambo)
16 Bolero Back Spot Turn (Mambo)

Bolero Silver Figures

1. Open Check Back half of basic, right foot side to forward open break, close to right foot side lunge (lady under arm turn right), forward walk to left side lunge (lady side step to right foot back check), close to cross body, back half of basic.

2. Overturned Cross Body Lead back half of basic, right foot side to forward open break, left foot side to cross body lead, right foot side and pivot turn (lady left foot side step and back break), left foot side to cross body lead, right foot side and head loop pivot turn to left (Lady left foot side step and back break), left foot side step to right foot lunge, Left foot side step to back break (lady right foot side step to under arm turn right), right foot side step back half of basic.

3. Rondé, Pass Behind the Back 2nd half of basic, right foot side to forward open break, left foot side to back spot turn (lady quick under arm turn left to back spot turn), right foot lunge (lady right foot ronde and back step to side step behind man's back), Left foot forward swivel and right foot check (lady right foot forward swivel and left foot check), right foot side step to left foot contra check and recover (lady quick under arm turn left-to-right foot contra check and recover).

4. Curl, Fan, Lunge Starts with right foot side to forward open break, left foot side step to right foot side lunge and recover (lady under arm turn left and left foot forward to ronde and right foot forward walk), three forward walks turning right (lady left foot side step to syncopated Fallaway grapevine), swivel on right foot to left foot side lunge then right foot side lunge (lady swivel on right foot to left foot forward lunge the right foot back lunge), Position held for SW then left foot forward step (lady position held for S then cross body lead), forward half of basic.

Summary: Open break, curl, lunge away for fan, twist back together, opening out (walk around), swivel for lady, lunge to left, lunge to right, Crossbody turning to the left in closed.

5. Spin Wrap right-to-right hand hold, forward open break, left foot close to right foot side lunge (lady right foot side to under arm turn right), three forward walks turning right (lady right foot spin to left foot forward ronde and right foot forward walk), left foot side and right foot toned to cross behind the left foot side step (lady left foot forward check to syncopated under arm turn left), forward right foot side step and under arm turn right (lady back half of basic), left foot side step and cross body lead, forward half of basic.

6. Shadow Checks begins in cross hand hold, Forward open break, SQ&Q left foot side lung to under arm turn right (lady right foot sit check to under arm turn left), left foot side lunge to right foot side lunge (lady right foot sit check to under arm turn right), Underarm spin left right foot forward check and recover(lady left foot forward to right foot forward check and recover), right foot forward with head loop to left foot forward check and recover (lady same), &SQ&Q left foot back and right foot point hold for Q then two forward walks (lady left foot side step and the syncopated free spin right), forward half of basic.

7. Walks & Fan begins open facing partner double hand hold, 1st half of basic, left foot back with right foot point to 2 back walks (lad right foot forward swivel and 2 forward walks), right foot side lunge and 2 back walks (Lady left foot forward swivel and 2 forward walks), left foot side lung right foot side lunge left foot side lunge (lady right foot forward swivel left foot forward swivel to set check, right foot forward swivel to sit check), right foot forward spin to left foot side lunge and recover (lady left foot side step and 2 forward walks), left foot back replace and close (lady right foot forward and swivel under arm turn left), forward half of basic.

8. Checked Pass, Hip Twist & Spin forward half of basic, 1 Measures back spot turn in in cradle position (lady 2 forward walks and right foot side step), right foot forward spin to forward check (lady left foot side step to back check), left foot side lung to cross body lead (lady right foot forward swivel to syncopated solo spin to left), forward half of basic.

9. Cross-Over, Quick Sit & Rumba Rock starts with an open break, underarm pass with underarm turn, cross over break with overturned underarm turn on the return, spiral turn partner back the other direction, step forward and swivel, forward side back, rumba rocks, step and swivel, circular walk around the lady.

10. Slow Spiral & Swivel back half of basic, forward open break, point left foot to side and hold (lady completes spiral turn S swivel on right foot swivel on left foot), hold S FL side lunge on Q hold Q (lady swivel on right foot swivel on left foot hold), right foot side step, left foot side and ronde right foot behind (lady right foot forward step, left foot forward and pivot then right foot back), forward half of basic.

11. One Leg Open Break. This is a style change for the open break. Instead of rocking back on the open break, lead partner to rock back while lowering on the right leg and sliding the left leg out to the side.

Mambo

Mambo is a fast dance characterized by strong Cuban Motion, staccato movement and expression of rhythm through the body. The dancer holds on count "1" and breaks on count "2."

The footwork for Mambo is Ball Flat throughout, but it is acceptable to dance "back breaks" using just the ball of the foot without lowering the heel. This technique prevents the upper body from falling back and allows the dancer to keep up with the speed of the music. Toes should be slightly turned out and feet should be kept in contact with the floor.

Steps should be staccato and striking. Incorporate strong rib action with the Cuban Motion. The hip motion, rather than "rolling," is sharper and uses a "twisting" action on each step. A "press-line" (a delayed weight transfer) makes for attractive leg lines and allows dancers to keep up with the music. This technique is optional. Because count "1" is the strong, downbeat of the Measure, the body should express this beat by using strong hip and rib cage action, even though there is no weight change.

Stand with body weight poised over the center of the feet to create connection with partner. Maintain same height throughout the dance, keeping the head erect and shoulders relaxed away from the ears. Avoid tilting the shoulders from side to side.

Use Cuban Motion, being sure to step with the knee flexed and to delay straightening. Keep ribcage lifted and moving in opposition from the hips. Take small steps. Lead and follow from the center of the body, using compression and leverage. Use the free arm in a natural way to complement the music and body movement.

While many figures in this syllabus begin with a Cross-Body Lead, note that this entrance may be eliminated.

Timing for Mambo is 234 where the 1 does not have a foot change. Mambo is very similar to Salsa. Most Salsa figures can be used in Mambo and Mambo figures can be used in Salsa.

Mambo Bronze Figures

1. Forward & Back Basic 1st half: left foot forward, replace weight to right foot, left foot slightly back from right foot. 2nd half: right foot back, replace weight to left foot, right foot slightly forward of left foot. under arm turn for follower can be lead when leader is going back and follower is going forward.

2. Side Breaks closed position or facing position or double hand hold, Side, replace weight, close, then the same on the other side.

3. Side Breaks & Cross closed position, 1st half: left foot side, replace weight to right foot slightly back, left foot crosses in front of right foot, 2nd half: right foot side, replace weight to left foot slightly back, right foot crosses in front of left foot.

4. Cross Body Lead closed position, 1st half: right foot forward, replace weight to right foot preparing right angle position turning 1/8 left, left foot side in right angle position turning 1/8 left, 2nd half: right foot side pivot ¼ turn left end right foot back, replace weight to left foot, right foot forward small step. Follower is led forward in front of leader as the leader turns.

5. Open Break Underarm Turn closed position, cross body lead ending in Facing position, open break end side, right foot back break (5th position break) end side (lady spot under arm turn right).

6. Crossover Break & Walk Around closed position, cross body lead ending side (prep left side partner), left foot crossover break end side, right foot solo spot turn to left end side in closed position (partner does solo spot turn to the R).

7. Shoulder Check cross body lead to Facing position, open break and prep for shoulder check (follower's under arm turn left, leader stops rotation of the turn by placing right hand on partner's left shoulder blade), forward check across partner's path (the shoulder check) and return to Facing position unwinding partner's previous turn.

8. Promenade Swivel & Close closed position, cross body lead, open break to prep follower's walk around turn, two forward walks and side step changing places (follower OS under arm turn right), left foot back break in Fallaway position (5th position) end side, swivel on left foot then forward side close.

9. Alternating Underarm Turns closed position, cross body lead to Facing position, open break prep Funder arm turn right, right foot back for 5th position break (follower spot under arm turn right), change of hands for spot under arm turn right (follower right foot back break), change of hands for right foot back for 5th position break (follower spot under arm turn right).

10. Rueda Basic closed position, cross body lead, left foot back break in Fallaway position end side, swivel to promenade position then forward side back (grapevine) end in left side partner, left foot back break in left side partner left foot forward swivel end in Facing position, right foot forward break in Facing position right foot back in left side partner, repeat Measures 5 and 6, left foot back break in left side partner left foot forward prop follower's spot under arm turn right, back break (follower spot under arm turn right)

11. Cross Body Lead with Inside Turn closed position, 1st half of cross body lead, 2nd half of cross body lead with follower's progressive pivot under arm turn left.

12. Back Spot Turn closed position cross body lead end right foot side in Facing position, open break left foot side, three Measures of back spot turn beginning right foot behind and ending right foot closed, left foot back break in Fallaway position end left foot closed, right foot side break.

13. Mambo Twist closed position, left foot side break left foot hook right leg ronde (lady back break, swivel, hip twist), right foot back side close (left outside position).

14. Forward Spot Turn to Surprise closed position, cross body lead with forward spot turn ending, left foot forward check and replace and side (the surprise) (follower right foot side break and swivel), back side close (left outside position).

15. Crossover Swivels & Pullback closed position, cross body lead ending side (prep left side partner), left foot crossover break swivel to left, swivel to right swivel to left and pull back a4, swivel right swivel left prep left side partner, repeat crossover and swivels, left foot cross over break end side (prep Funder arm turn right), right foot back break (follower spot under arm turn right)

Mambo Silver Figures

1. Cross Body Lead Variations for Man & Lady:
   A. Man Flick add flick of right foot on 1 of the 1st half of cross body lead.
   B. Man Check right foot side check on back half
   C. Lady Roll hip roll for lady on the 1st half
   D. Lady Cross & Twist cross and twist for lady on the 1st half
   E. Lady Knee Lift knee lift for lady on the 1st half

2. Underarm Turn & Traveling Cross Open break, right foot back break (lady under arm turn right), open break (lady open break to under arm turn left), side cross side (lady under arm turn left).

3. Bobby's Break open facing partner left-to-right hand hold, open break (lady open break and under arm turn left), back spot turn, left foot forward walk to side break right (the Bobby's break) (lady back walk, side break left and knee lift), second half of cross body lead, left foot forward offset check (lady side break) ronde (lady forward swivel OP), back half of box with lady OP.

4. Continuous Cross Body Leads 1st half of cross body lead and right foot forward kick, back half of box and left foot forward lock (lady solo turn to left and right foot forward kick), solo turn to left and right foot forward kick (lady back half of box and left foot forward kick), repeat previous two Measures, three forward walks (lady 2nd half of cross body lead). Figure can be done in place as described or progressive.

5. Back Spot Spin & Check open break, back spot turn to swivel (lady back spot turn to quick under arm turn right), left foot forward break (lady right foot back break) end in tandem position, cross side forward end in shadow position (lady cross side back), left foot forward break (lady right foot back break and hip roll, 2nd half of cross body lead.

6. Salsa Wrap open break, right foot back break for lady under arm turn right while man turns right maintaining a two-hand hold to create a wrap position. Then a forward check and a left turn to lead partner to unwrap during a crossover break. Then leader does a 270 turn under his own arm to end at 90 to his partner followed by a left side cross body lead with underarm turn.

7. Double Face Loop open break to side step (lady open break to quick under arm turn left), head loop and two steps of back spot turn forward step (lady two forward walks turning right to side step)- all previous with man turning to right, left foot side break side step (lady back break to quick under arm turn left), head loop and two forward walks to side step-man now turning right, 5th position break, box ending from promenade position.

8. Shadow Break open break, right foot back break to forward walk (lady overturned under arm turn right end in shadow position), left foot forward break (lady right foot back break), right foot back break to forward walk (lady overturned under arm turn right end in shadow position), left foot forward break (lady right foot back break), repeat previous two Measures, right foot back break to forward walk with head loop (lady double under arm turn left), 1st half of cross body lead, 2nd half of cross body lead.

9. Hammerlock & Swivels open break, right foot back break (lady under arm turn right and spin), open break to side step (lady back break side step turning left), swivels, swivels, right foot back break to side step (lady left foot forward check to under arm turn left).

10. Jazz Boxes are forward side back, back side forward making 180 turn. In closed hold, turn 1/8 to the right step forward, turn ½ turn to the right and step back turning an 1/8 now start the next side of the box, back turning 1/8, step side turning ¼, step forward turning an 1/8

11. Back Cuban Break from closed position lead partner to do a back rock while doing a cucaracha, then do lead two back rocks for partner while leader also does back rocks.

12. Crab Walks start in promenade position with inside foot moving forward, turn to face partner and take a side step, turn back to promenade position then inside foot moves forward.

13. Same Foot Lunge In two hand hold, step back to a split weight position and lower while leading partner with an active top rotation to slide one foot between your legs. This position can be held for a count or two for effect. Lead back to square position when finished.

Mambo commonly uses many hand-hold positions for setting up turns. **A general rule is the in a cross-hand hold with the left hand on top needs a pass to the left side while using the hand positions to make appropriate turns. A cross hand hold with the right hand on top will need a right-side pass while using the hand positions to make appropriate turns**

Samba

Samba is an upbeat, lively dance that progresses counter-clockwise around the floor. It is characterized by its bounce and rolling hip action. The count is 1a2, 1a2. Beat Value: 3/4-1/4-1, 3/4-1/4-1 (the "a" count is equal to 1/4 of a beat of music).

Most figures are danced: Ball Flat, Ball, Ball Flat. Maintain slight turn out of the feet. Keep feet in contact with the floor.

Emphasize the syncopated timing (1 a2) by holding the first step 3/4 of a beat before changing weight. The second step, count "a", will therefore be very short (1/4 of a beat). The third step (count 2), is then held for a full beat. Use correct Samba bounce, being sure to flex and straighten the knees. The bounce in Samba is danced evenly (1/2 beat for the flexing, and 1/2 beat for the straightening), in contrast to the syncopated timing of the steps. The bounce should emphasize the downward movement to create an earthy feel. Advanced technique incorporates a forward and back movement of the hips and pelvis which adds body rhythm and absorbs the rise so that the dancer does not rise above standing height. A great deal of rhythm is expressed though the torso, which should remain flexible.

Stand with a forward poise to create connection with partner. Lead and follow from the center of the body, using compression and leverage. Use the free arm in a natural way to complement the music and body movement.

Samba Bronze American

1 a 2 3 a 4 for the steps (a is 1/4), 1 & 2 3 & 4 for the bounce (& is 1/2)

1. Basic Bounce described above.
2. Forward & Back Basic left foot forward, right foot closes to left foot, replace weight to left foot, right foot back, left foot closes to right foot, replace weight to right foot
3. Side to Side Basic left foot side, right foot closes to left foot, replace weight to left foot, right foot side, left foot closes to right foot, replace weight to left foot.
4. Fifth Position left foot side right foot 5th position break, right foot side left foot 5th position break.
5. Box forward side close, back side close.
6. Extended Box forward side close, side close side, back side close, side close side.
7. Samba Walks 5th position breaks in promenade position, left foot samba walk in promenade position, right foot samba walks in promenade position, twinkle for

promenade position to closed position, then forward and back basic. A Samba Walk is forward then rock back with some weight to the other foot pulling back a bit on the first step and then a full weight transfer to the first step.

8. Forward & Back Spiral (Boto Fogos) left foot forward Boto Fogo to right outside partner, right foot forward Boto Fogo from right outside partner to left outside position, left foot forward Boto Fogo to right outside partner, right foot forward twinkle from right outside partner to closed position.

Detail of Boto Fogo
On "1" step forward with the left foot slightly diagonally across the body (i.e., step in CBMP) On "a" step sideways with partial weight transfer. During this and the next steps, make a quarter turn to the left. On "2" replace the full weight onto the left foot.

9. Reverse Samba Walk 5th position break ending in outside closed position, right foot samba walks in left side partner, left foot samba walk in facing position, right foot samba walk in left side partner, twinkle from left side partner to closed position, 2nd half of box.

10. Promenade & Counter Promenade Boto Fogos left foot forward Boto Fogo from closed position to promenade position, right foot forward Boto Fogo from closed position to promenade position, twinkle from promenade position to closed position.

11. Opening Out Left & Right, left foot Boto Fogo to left outside position, right foot Boto Fogo to right outside position, left foot Boto Fogo to left outside position, right foot Boto Fogo to right outside position.

12. Rolling Box 1st half a box with rolling action turning left, 2nd half a box with rolling action turning left, 1st half a box with rolling action turning left, 2nd half a box with rolling action turning left, making one or two full turns in 4 Measures.

13. Volta to Left & Right Voltas are like a forward basic with the first step crossing in front of the other foot. Because of the crossover action, a series of Voltas may be easily curved or done in a straight line. Changing directions in a Volta series is done by crossing the back foot over the front.

14. Open Break 5th position break to the left, right foot side open break. This is the lead in for a spot turn.

15. Advanced Left Turn T is like a Volta that turns 3/8 turn to the left on each 1a2.

Samba American Bronze Variations

1 Open break and under arm turn (Mambo)
2 Shoulder Check (Mambo)
3 Promenade Swivel and Close (Mambo)
4 Alternating under arm turns (Mambo)

5 Crossbody lead with under arm turn (Mambo)
6 Flip Flops (Foxtrot)

Samba International Bronze

1A. Natural Basic right foot forward, left foot closes to right foot without weight, left foot back, right foot closes to left foot without weight.
1B. Reverse Basic same as basic started with the left foot
1C. Side Basic left foot side, right foot closes to left foot, replace weight to left foot, right foot side, left foot closes to right foot, replace weight to left foot.
1D. Progressive Basic 1st half of right foot forward basic, 1st half of left foot side basic, like a waltz progressive
2. Whisks to Left and Right left foot side right foot 5th position break, right foot side left foot 5th position break.
3A. Promenade Samba Walks A Samba Walk is forward then rock back with some weight to the other foot pulling back a bit on the first step and then a full weight transfer to the first step.
3B. Side Samba Walks right foot forward, left foot side with some weight, draw right foot slightly towards left foot.
3C. Stationary Samba Walks left foot closes to right foot, right foot back part weight, draw left foot slightly towards right foot, right foot closes to left foot slightly forward, left foot back part weight, draw right foot slightly forward towards left foot.
4. Rhythm Bounce a - swing pelvis softly in the direction of the free leg, 1 - swing pelvis softly in the direction of the standing leg.
5. Volta Movements to Left & Right Voltas are like a forward basic with the first step crossing in front of the other foot (a Cuban cross), rocking back with some weight to the back foot and then full weight to the crossing foot. Because of the crossover action, a series of Voltas may be easily curved or done in a straight line. Changing directions in a Volta series is done by crossing the back foot over the front.
6. Traveling Bota Fogos Forward right foot forward outside partner, left foot to side with part weight, replace weight to right foot turning ¼ right on the three steps, left foot forward outside partner on partner's left side, right foot to side part weight, replace weight to left foot turning ¼ turn left on the three steps.
7. Criss Cross Bota Fogos left foot forward Boto Fogo to right outside partner, right foot forward Boto Fogo from right outside partner to left outside partner position, left foot forward Boto Fogo to right outside partner, right foot forward twinkle from right outside partner to closed position.
8. Traveling Bota Fogos Back Same as 6 starting back instead of forward.

9. Bota Fogos to Promenade and Counter Promenade left foot forward Boto Fogo from closed position to promenade position, right foot forward Boto Fogo from closed position to promenade position, twinkle from promenade position to closed position.

10. Criss Cross Voltas Dance 2 bars of traveling Voltas to R, curving behind lady's back, dance 2 bars of traveling Voltas to L, curving behind lady's back to end in closed position.

11. Solo Spot Voltas Same as step 5 with one full turn over the 1a2.

12. Foot Changes A kick, a tap or doing 1 2 instead of 1a2 will change leader's feet to match partner's for shadow or side-by-side.

13. Shadow Traveling Voltas Same as traveling Voltas after a foot change.

14. Reverse Turn left foot forward, right foot to side and slightly back, left foot crosses in front of right foot toe turned out making 3/8 left turn in these three steps, right foot back and slightly right, left heel close to right heel, right foot closes to left foot making ½ left turn in these three steps.

15. Corta Jaca 12&1&2&right foot forward, left foot forward slightly to the side, right foot slide leftwards, left foot back and slightly to side, right foot slides leftwards, Left foot forward and slightly to side, right foot slides leftwards.

16. Closed Rocks 12&12& right foot forward, left foot forward, replace weight to right foot, left foot forward small step, right foot forward, replace weight to left foot.

Samba International Silver

17. Open Rocks 12&12& right foot forward, left foot forward, replace weight to right foot, left foot forward, right foot forward, replace weight to left foot.

18. Back Rocks 12&12& right foot back, rock left foot forward and slightly leftwards completing ¼ turn to the left, rock back to right foot, left foot back and slightly rightwards completing ¼ turn to the right.

19. Plait QQSSSQQS right foot back twisting, left foot back twisting, continue for the count.

20. Rolling Off the Arm Whisk to the left LRL, whisk to the right RLR.

21 Argentine Crosses left foot forward toe turned out, right foot behind left foot toe turned out turning R, left foot to side and slightly forward completing ¼ turn to the right, right foot forward in front of left foot small step toe turned out, left foot to side and slightly back turning R, right foot forward in front of left foot small step toe turned out completing ¼ turn to the right.

22 Maypole Commence in Open promenade position, left-to-right hand hold, use bounce action. Man dances a circular Volta around while partner dances a spot Volta turning the other direction.

23. Shadow Circular Volta in shadow position, dance a circular Volta.

Paso Doble

Paso Doble is marching like dance. It is characterized by an exaggerated bull fighter like posture maintained during the dance since the dance is designed to be a bit like a bull fight with the man as the bull fighter and the lady as the bull. It is commonly danced to three songs that all have the same structure which allows the dancers to choreograph dance routines to include a highlight (big flourish) into the routine.

Paso Doble Bronze

1. **Surplace** eight steps in in place to beat of the music
2. **Basic Movement** Danced in closed position on the balls of the feet, heels may be lightly lowered, knees slightly flexed.
3. **The Appel** Danced in place on either foot with a strong lowering action with the foot flat. The appel is counted &1.
4. **Chassés to Right,** right foot to side, left foot closes to right foot, right foot to side, left foot closes to right foot.
5. **Chassés to Left,** left foot to side, right foot closes to left foot, left foot to side, right foot closes to left foot.
6. **Drag** flex left knee, right foot to side wide step knee flexed, commence closing left foot to right foot slowly straighten right knee, close left foot to right foot.
7. **Deplacement** right foot forward, left foot forward, right foot to side, left foot closes to right foot.
8. **Promenade Link** Appel on right foot, left foot to side in promenade position, right foot forward and across in promenade position and CBMP, left foot closes to right foot.
9. **Promenade** appel on right foot, left foot to side in promenade position, right foot forward and across in promenade position and CBMP, left foot to side and slightly back, right foot back, left foot back, right foot to side and slightly forward, left foot closes to right foot.
10. **Ecart** appel right foot, left foot forward, right foot to side and slightly back in Fallaway, left foot crosses behind right foot in Fallaway.
11. **Separation** appel on right foot, left foot forward, right foot closes to left foot, Sur Place left foot, 4 sur place RLRL.
12. **Separation with Lady's Caping Walks** appel on right foot, left foot forward, right foot closes to left foot, sur place left foot 4 sur place RLRL, 9-14 hold position feet together while lady capes around, right foot side, left foot closes to right foot.
13. **Fallaway Ending to Separation** right foot forward OP, left foot forward OP, right foot back and slightly side in Fallaway, left foot back in Fallaway and

CBMP, right foot side, left foot closes to right foot, right foot to side, left foot closes to right foot.

14. Huit right foot forward and across in promenade position and CBMP, left foot closes to right foot, 3-8 Sur Place RLRLRL while partner …

15. Sixteen Appel right foot, left foot side in promenade position, right foot forward and across in promenade position and CBMP, Left foot to side a slightly back, right foot back preparing to lead partner outside, left foot back in CBMP, right foot closes to left foot, sur place left foot , 9-16 sur place RLRLRLRL.

16. Promenade and Counter Promenade appel on right foot, left foot side in promenade position, right foot forward and across in promenade position and CBMP, left foot back and slightly side, right foot to side in closed position, left foot forward and across in closed position and CBMP, right foot forward and slight to side, FO side in promenade position.

17. Grand Circle right foot forward and across in promenade position and CBMP, 2-8 twist to left with feet in place ending with left foot forward in promenade position weight on left foot, right foot forward and across in promenade position and CBMP, left foot closes to right foot.

18. Open Telemark slip appel right foot, left foot forward, right foot side, Left foot side and slightly back in promenade position, right foot forward and across in promenade position and CBMP, left foot closes to right foot, right foot side, left foot closes to right foot. Figure turns 7/8 turn left over the 8 beats.

Paso Doble Silver

19. La Passe 1-5 first five steps of sixteen, left foot back in CBMP partner outside, right foot forward, 89 hesitate with weight on right foot, left foot forward, 11-12 hesitate with weight on left foot, right foot forward, 14-15 hesitate with weight on right foot, left foot closes to right foot.

20. Banderillas sur place 1-4 RLR, appel on right foot, left foot to side wide step, right foot closes to left foot moving to lady's right side almost hip to hip, surplace left foot, right foot forward OSP, left foot to side small step with partner in line, right foot closes to left foot, surplace left foot.

21. Twist Turn 1-4 steps of sixteen, right foot crosses loosely behind left foot, 6-7 twist both feet right 1.5 turn, end with weight on right foot

22. Fallaway Reverse Turn slip appel right foot, left foot forward, right foot to side and slightly back in CBMP and Fallaway, right foot back, replace weight forward to left foot, right foot to side, left foot closes to right foot. 7/8 turn left over figure.

23. Coup de Pique point right foot forward and across in promenade position and CBMP without weight left knee flexed, right foot closes to left foot, left foot back in Fallaway and CBMP, right foot closes to left foot, left foot back in Fallaway and CBMP, right foot side, left foot closes to right foot, right foot side, left foot closes to right foot.

24. Left foot Variation left foot forward, right foot forward, left foot forward preparing to step OP on right side, point right foot forward without weight OP left knee flexed, left foot closes to right foot, right foot side, left foot closes to right foot.

25. Spanish Lines right foot forward and across in promenade position, left foot side, right foot back in closed position, left foot forward and slightly across right foot without weight but slight pressure left knee flexed, left foot forward, right foot side, left foot back promenade position, right foot forward and slightly across left foot without weight with slight pressure right knee flexed.

26. Flamenco Taps danced from a Spanish Line, replace weight forward to the left foot, tap right foot behind left foot twice 2&, right foot back small step, right foot back small step, Place left foot into Spanish line position.

Night Club Dances

West Coast Swing

West Coast Swing is smooth (no bounce) and danced in a slot. **This dance allows room for syncopated footwork and improvisation**. West Coast Swing can be danced to a wide range of music including rhythm and blues, country western, funk, disco, rock and pop.

The basic count is 12, 3a4, 5a6 with a beat value: 1-1, 3/4-1/4-1, 3/4-1/4-1. West coast swing is commonly taught as 12 3&4 5&6 for six count patterns and 12 3&4 56 7&8 for eight count patterns.

In the swing dances, the "a" count is equal to 1/4 of a beat of music before the beat that follows the "a". The footwork is ball flat throughout except the first step of a forward running triple is ball. Forward steps may be taken as heel flat. Taps can be used depending on styling and placement of foot. Taps may be taken on the inside edge of the toe, inside edge of the ball, on the ball, or on the heel. Toes should be slightly turned out. Keep feet in contact with the floor.

A Side Triple travels sideways, either to the right or left with a side, close, side movement.

An Anchor Triple is the last triple step of most WCS figures. Anchor triples are usually danced in place, allowing partners to re-establish leverage. The Post is the step before the anchor triple which establishes the relative position of the partners for the anchor triple. West Coast swing provides a lot of room to be play full and the Post and Anchor are used to close out one figure to set up for the start of the next figure.

A Forward running triple is a triple in which the feet pass on each step. The Follower's first triple step of a side pass is a forward running triple, as are steps 3-5 of the Underarm Turn.

A Delayed Forward Triple is a triple whose first two steps are in place and the third is forward. Occasionally danced by Followers, it is mostly danced by Leaders, as in steps 3-5 of the Left Side Pass.

A Delayed Back Triple is triple whose first two steps are in place and the third is back. Followers dance these more than Leaders, as on steps 3-5 of the Sugar Push.

A Delayed Side Triple is a triple whose first two steps are in place and the third is side. Leaders dance these more often than Followers as in steps 3-5 of the Basic Whip.

A Hook Triple is a triple whose first step is one foot stepping behind the other with the toe turned out. Foot positions for steps 2 and 3 vary depending on the figure. The Leader dances a hook triple on steps 6-8 of the Underarm turn with Leader's Loop and Right-Side Pass.

A Back-Closing Triple, also called a coaster step, is a triple whose three steps are back, close, and forward. This is occasionally danced by Leaders, but mostly Followers dance back closing triples, as on steps 3-5 of the Basic Whip.

West coast swing is danced in the slot, in other words back and forth on line. The Follower should place the moving foot in the same track as the standing foot to maintain a narrow slot. During anchor triples, the Leader and Follower settle weight away from each other (i.e., create leverage) in preparation for the next figure.

The Follower should not step forward until led on count 1. Depending on the style of WCS danced, swing hip action may or may not be used. The closed position in swing is a dance position where the Leader's right side and Follower's left side are almost in contact and the opposite sides are open in a very slight V- shape. The Leader's left hand is held at Follower's waist level in a cup position, and the Follower's right-hand hooks lightly over the Leader's hand. The Leader's right hand is placed on the Follower's left shoulder blade, and the Follower's left-hand rests on the Leader's right shoulder. The Follower should be slightly offset to the Leader's right.

Maintain same height throughout the dance, keeping the head erect and shoulders relaxed. Do not tilt the shoulders. Take small steps. Lead and follow from the center of the body, using leverage and compression. Style the free arm in a natural way from the core to complement the music and body movement.

The good WC Swing dancers roll through the feet creating body flight like in Smooth. The difference is that this motion is commonly back and forth. **The spine is kept moving by rolling the weight through the foot (back to front or front to back) of the standing leg and moving the pelvis forward or back to create a continuous movement of the body while on the standing leg.**

West Coast Swing Bronze

Timing on six count patterns is 1 2, 3a4, 5a6 and 1 2, 3a4, 5 6, 7a8 on eight count patterns. Emphasis is on even counts. The dance usually starts in closed position with side triples or side to side rocking steps and then moves out to mostly open steps (see step 7) below.

1. Underarm Turn Starts in open facing position 12 left foot back right foot forward in front of left foot raising left hand rightward turning 1/8 to the right, 3a4 Side triple turning 4/8 turn right while follower does under arm turn left, 5a6 anchor triple. The leader ends the under arm turn slightly offset to the left side of the slot which makes it possible to lead consecutive underarm turns. In order to lead a left side pass or other left side figures, the leader needs to adjust the steps on 3a45 end on the right side of the slot prepared to have follower pass on the left side.

2. Left Side Pass 12 left foot back right foot side turning ¼ turn left guiding partner to pass on left side, 3a4 delayed forward triple turning another ¼ turn to left while follower does a forward running triple, 5a6 Anchor triple.

3. Sugar Push 12 left foot back and close taking double hand hold and begin slight body rotation to the right, 3a4 delayed forward triple (left foot closes to right foot, replace weight to right foot, left foot forward creating the post position), 5a6 anchor triple.

4. (Underarm Turn to) Right Side Pass 12 back replace turn 1/8 right, 3a4 triple in place turning 1/8 right leading under arm turn left for partner end in right-to-right hand hold in RAP, 5a6 triple in place, 12 side replace and regain left-to-right hand hold, 3a4 delayed forward triple with ¼ turn L, anchor triple in open facing position.

5. Tuck-In from Left Side Pass 12 left foot back right foot back in double hand hold with ¼ turn to right in right angle position, 3a4 1/8 turn left delayed forward triple leading follower a little right for the tuck then left for the inside turn under arm turn right on 4 releasing your right hand, 5a6 anchor triple.

6. Tuck-In from Right Side Pass 12 3a4 5a6 for and under arm turn figure 1 end in right-to-right hand hold, 12 left foot back right foot side in right-to-right hand hold with ¼ turn left, 3a4 delayed forward triple prep follower's spin on a, on 4 rotate 1/8 left leading follower's spin, 5a6 anchor triple.

7. Half Whip and Throw Out/Starter Step 12 back and replace turning 1/8 turn right ending in right angle position, 3a4 turning triple to the right 3/8 turn end in Swing closed position, 5a6 side triple turning ¼ right.
The throw out is 12 opening out, 3a4 delated forward triple turning ¼ turn left, 5a6 anchor triple.
A starter step is a triple to the left and triple to the right or sways left, right, left, right followed by a throw out or a lead into a whip of some sort. A starter step is

Clarke Fairbrother – Dance Nuggets

only used at the beginning of the dance. When a figure ends in closed position the leader immediately dances a throw out instead of a starter step.

8. Basic Whip Starts in open facing position, 12 back and replace, 3a4 delayed side triple turning right starting in right angle position and ending in Swing closed position, 56 side, side, 7a8 anchor step in open facing position.

9. Whip with Inside Turn Same as the whip with follower inside under arm turn left on count 5.

10. Whip with Outside Turn Same as the whip with follower outside under arm turn right on count 5. This turn can easily become a double turn for follower.

11. Whip with Check 12 back replace, 3a4 delayed side triple end in side lunge in right angle position while follower does a forward check, 56 replace and side, 7a8 Anchor steps

12. Underarm Turn with Leader's Loop to Right Side Pass 12 back & replace, 3a4 delayed forward triple turning right with follower doing under arm turn left, 5a6 loop turn right (hook triple) ending in right-to-right hand hold (the leader's loop), followed by a right-side pass 123a45a6.

13. Sugar Push Point in open facing position, 12 back close, 4a5 tap & forward, a56 syncopated anchor triple (close point hold).

14. Lock Whip or Basket Whip, first half of basic whip in double hand hold ending in right side cradle position (no turn for partner), followed by 2nd half of a basic whip.

15. Continuous Whip 123a4, first half of a basic whip, 56 forward side with ¼ turn right in Swing closed position, 78 forward side with a ¼ turn right. 78 can be repeated a longer whip. To exit the turning whip, step forward on 1 and 23a4 end of basic whip.

Variations for social dancing from EC Swing
Alternating under arm turns # 8
Double Face Loop # 13
Opposition break and roll out #14

West Coast Swing Silver

1. Checked Whip and Throw-out 1234567&8, Checked whip, checked whip with throw-out.
2. Roll In and Pass 12a345&6, Back break with lady forward, side cross turning right with lady rolling in, forward walk, cross triple in place.
3. Double Face Loop, Tuck Spin Back break with lady forward walks, side triple to left with lady under arm turn left, side triple right with right- and left-hand head loops.
4. Man's Hammerlock and Tummy Whip 123&45&6, Back break with lady two forward walks, side triple to left turn right with lady under arm turn left, turning cross triple with hand change behind the back while lady triples in place, 1234567&8, Back break turning right while lady walks forward, whip turn with lady's syncopated forward break step and 2 backward walks, cross triple in place.
5. Lock Whip, Side Break and Spin 12 3&4 56 7&8, Back break with lady coming forward, side triple to left turning right to end in cradle position, cross behind, forward with lady's under arm turn right, cross triple in place ending in hammerlock position with lady under arm spin to the right, 12 4&4 5&6, forward step to side lunge ending in left side partner with lady forward step to side lunge left, side triple with lady's solo spin right, side triple right with lady's side triple left, 12 3&4 5&6, opposition break, back triple in place with lady's running triple, cross triple in place.
6. Spinning Hammerlock Left side pass to tuck in, forward walk and cross triple in place with lady under arm turn and spin right, end in hammerlock position, 2 steps of left side pass, forward triple in place and head loop with lady under arm turn left, cross triple in place.
7. Continuous Whip Basic whip pivots without & counts, cross check with lady back break and cross triple with lady double under arm turn right to end.
8. Sugar Push Syncopations 123&456, adds a kick on count 5.
9. Underarm Turn Syncopations 123&456, adds a kick on count 5.
10. Roll In, Check & Throw out 12&345&6, left foot back break, running triple turning right while lady rolls in, right foot forward check and close with lady's syncopated back break and close. 123&45&6, left foot side break with lady's right foot back break, back closing triple with lady running triple, cross triple in place.
11. Hammer lock tuck from sugar push. (not syllabus) At the end of the 4 in the sugar push, raise the left hand as if to do an underarm turn on the way back, but hold on to the other hand to create a hammer lock position. Lead underarm turn or spin to unwind from hammer lock position.
12. Swivel walks from hammer lock (not syllabus) From the hammerlock position created in the previous figure now swivel partner back and forth in

hammerlock position. Lead underarm turn or spin to unwind from hammer lock position.

13. Hustle Whip with shoulder roll, (not syllabus) starts as whip but instead of capturing partner for the turn back out of the whip, let her continue to move away while doing an arm slide to two hand hold. This part is the Hustle Whip. From the two-hand hold lead partner for a UAT with the right hand while turning left under your own arm (the shoulder roll), roll out of these turns in right hand side-by-side-by-side position. Roll partner in and hook step for a 180 turn and roll partner out, do three of these, rolling partner out with a double spin to anchor on the last roll out.

14 Cha Cha Step (not syllabus) Sugar push start, turn ¼ to R, forward lock triple step, 180 turn away from partner, forward lock back triple back to the slot, both turn inside, post and anchor.

West Coast Swing Alternate pushes and passes

1. Inside Turning Sugar Push Six count pattern, inside under arm turn for partner on 3&4, under arm turn left for leader on 5&6.

2. Head loop Pass Six count pattern, lead left side pass, as partner passes on 3&4 loop left hand over head while turning ½ turn to the right dropping partner's hand on your right shoulder so that she can trail the right arm, collect the follower in right-to-right hand hold for 5&6.

3. High-Five Pass right-to-right hand hold, six count pattern, bring follower down right side, prepping a under arm turn left by turning partner a little to the right on 12, bring right hand up leading outside under arm turn left on 3&4 turning ¼ turn right which will create the high five position, stop compress into lady leading her for a under arm turn right while turning ¼ turn right on 5&6 end with hand change back to left to R.

4. Same Side Tuck with Man's Behind the Back Hand Change left-to-right hand hold, six count pattern, 12 BB, 3 back with ball only (a ball change while partner checks), -a- replace weight, 4 forward creating a compression with partner for her pivot under arm turn right on the 45, 5 facing & facing 6 across while turning ¾ turn right for a behind the back hand change finishing right-to-right hand hold.

5. Shooting Gallery right-to-right hand hold, ten count pattern, 12 BB prep partner to right, 3&4 turn ¼ left rolling partner left into right side shadow position, 56 move partner to left side shadow leader does step tap follower does a tuning step together step, 78 move partner to the right side, leader does step tap follower does a turning step together step, 9&10 two hand illusion under arm turn right for partner to finish. The **illusion turn** starts in right-to-right left to left hand hold, turn follower to the right lifting the left hand over her head, place her left hand and leader's left hand on her right wrist, slip through the wrist picking up the hands of the other side, right hand over the head then the left hand over the head to complete the turn. In summary the hands go over the head left right left with the wrist illusion after the first turn.

6. Around the Push Regular sugar push with the push on 3 off to the leader's left with the follower circling around to in front of leader for 5&6.

7. Eggbeater Pass Start Double hand hold, six count pattern, leader's foot work is normal. Lead outside under arm turn right with left hand at the end of 1 and move the right hand through with the turn, slide the right hand down to partner's left arm pit turning the hand so that it is thumb down while looping left hand over your head as well as partner's, continue partner's rotation as she ducks under your right arm and continues her right turn, as she finishes her turn slide your right hand down her left arm to finish in right to left hand hold. Follower's steps are right foot forward pivot ½ turn right, left foot back pivot ½ turn right, right foot forward pivot ½ turn right, left foot closes to right foot, right foot back, then LRL for anchor step.

8. Wrap & Duck Pass Start right to left hand hold (as the last figure ended), six count pattern, as partner comes down your left side wrap her in as she turns left and she continues turning left under your arm and rolls out the other side changing hands to left-to-right hand hold and continuing the turn to the left to the anchor.

9. Over & Pop Out right-to-right hand hold, lead partner down left side leader making a under arm turn right for himself, follower also makes a turn to the right and ends up in hammerlock position, walks forward and anchors. Change to left-to-right hand hold at the end.

10. Behind the Neck & Through the Tunnel left-to-right hand hold 12 lead partner forward 3&4 take a side step and put hand on partner's shoulder to redirect her back where she came from 5&6 side step to lead to leaders left raising left hand to lead a both turn pivot turn, 78 step forward and then back to anchor.

West Coast Swing, other patterns

Rock and Go. This term describes putting two steps together eliminating the anchor between the two steps.

Salsa

Try to start dancing at the beginning of an 8-count phrase. Timing for Salsa is commonly 123_567_ where the 4 and 8 do not have a foot change. It can also be danced 234_ 678_ which is Mambo timing. Salsa is very similar to Mambo. Most Mambo figures can be used in Salsa. 23_5678_ is called Clave timing. There are other timings. Salsa dancers may vary their timing depending on the sounds in the music. Use Mambo figures with common elements below.

Forward & Back Basic left foot back, right foot back, left foot forward, right foot forward left foot forward right foot back or left foot forward, right foot back, left foot back a little not close, right foot back, left foot forward, right foot forward a little, not close.

Back Breaks Back, rock, together, like a 5th position break

Side Breaks Side, replace, together

Cross Body Lead Forward, back off the track dropping the left hand and leading the follower forward, side then back forward side

Turns The nose is the last to go and the first to return on all turns.

Basic Right Turn When turning right, step forward and to the right on the right foot turning the foot out to the right on the previous Measure, left foot side turning ¼ to the right, right foot replaces, turning ½ turn right, turn ¼ turn right stepping side.

Basic Left Turn is a mirror image of basic right turn.

Broken Left Turn 1 right foot forward, 2 left foot forward and across, 3 right foot back pivoting ½ turn to the left, 5 left foot forward pivoting ½ turn left, 6 right foot back 7 left foot forward.

½ Broken Left Turn 1 right foot forward, 2 left foot forward and across, 3 right foot back pivoting ½ turn to the left, 5 left foot forward, 6 right foot back, 7 left foot forward with a pivot ½ turn to the left.

Ladies Pivot Turn Right or left turn using a pivoting action (legs staying in a scissors position with movements being forward or back, not to the side).

Man's Hook Turn 5 left foot back, 6 right foot hook behind and with the knees flexed turn on the ball of the right foot and the heel of the left foot, 7 close left foot to right foot, this is the advanced twist turn method. This is also done 5 right foot hook behind turn ½ turn, 6 left foot step turn ½ turn, 7 right foot close.

Salsa Wrap - Open break, turn with hand change behind the back, basic in R to L HH, forward check with waist lead of cross body with spin, capture in closed hold.

Salsa Social Step – cross body lead to partner in front, opposing side checks, turn partner to face left side pass.

Spiral – cross body lead to cross hand hold, hands over heads, UAT while crossing to partners left.

Wrap to Right, roll in, roll out and dip.

Merengue

Merengue is a fun and easy dance made up of simple steps. This is the first dance taught on a cruise ship since stepping on every beat is easy to learn. Primarily a non-progressive dance, it can also travel counter-clockwise around the dance floor. Noted for its Cuban Motion, Merengue is also characterized by its marching feel. Emphasis may be put on count 1 by taking a larger step and slightly dragging the opposite/closing leg.

Footwork is Ball Flat through-out with the exception of taps. Depending on styling and placement of foot, taps can be taken inside edge of the toe, the inside edge of the ball of the foot, the ball of the foot, or the heel. Toes should be slightly turned out. Feet should stay in contact with the floor.

The Cuban Motion in Merengue is typically danced as more of a side to side action, rather than a rolling figure eight action.

Stand with the weight over the center of the standing foot with energy moving toward your partner to create connection. Maintain same height throughout the dance, keeping the spine long, the head up and shoulders down. Do not allow the shoulders to tilt from side to side. Use Cuban Motion, stepping with a flexed knee and delaying the straightening of the leg. Keep chest lifted and move the ribcage in opposition to the hips. Take small steps. Lead and follow from the center of the body, using compression and leverage. Keep the free arm alive (moving in a natural way that expresses the music and complements the body movement).

In addition to the Syllabus figures, you may also add forward walks (either straight or curving), backward walks, or marking time in place (with or without turn).

Merengue Bronze
1 2 3 4 5 6 7 8 with emphasis on the 1 and 5 counts

1. Merengue Basic to the Side starting with the left foot side chasses. The chasses may be curved to travel line of dance.
2. Back Rock from a side basic lead partner to turn to the right while leader turns to the left (creating Fallaway position) to do a 5th position break with the left foot.
3. Side Breaks alternating placing the foot to the side and closing.
4. Arm Slide While doing small back walks, slide the arms from closed position to Double hand hold position. Gradually lower then circle and extend the joined

hands out and up to the sides until the hands reach upward, then lower directly downward to regain closed position.

5. Back-to-back while marching in place arm slide hands up as in 4 above, start raising left hand lowering right hand. Leader and follower turn simultaneously under joined arms to end in back-to-back position with arms extended to the sides with double hand hold. Begin turning to the left by raising the right hand and lowering the left hand to turn under the joined arms back to facing and closed position.

6. Swivels, Straight and Turning change from, Fallaway position to promenade position and promenade position to closed position using compression in the frame to swivel both partners. Leader walks backwards while swiveling to convert this figure to turning.

7. Conga Breaks, Simple and Crossing Simple: 123a4, two walks in promenade position, right foot swivel to close left foot to right foot, then conga break in promenade position (right foot side, small step, tap left heel to side). For crossing: left foot side in promenade position, right foot forward and across then swivel promenade position to closed position, left foot forward and across in closed position, right foot side small step, tap left heel to side preparing promenade position to promenade position.

8. Merengue Glide Measure 1: basic to side. Measure 2: 5&6&78 syncopated chasses to side.

9. Forward Spot Turn Measure 1: 4 counts of forward spot turn, Measure 2 one count of forward spot turn, right foot side, and open break. **This is a right or natural turn.** Lead partner to block you and hook on her second step.

10. Back Spot Turn Measure 1 four counts of spot turn (left foot side, right foot hook), Measure two: left foot side, right foot close, opening out. **This is a left or reverse turn.** Lead by cutting off partner and inviting her to step between your legs on step 1.

11. Roll In & Out four counts of side basic, opening out left foot cross, right foot side ending left side partner (follower roll out), side cross side ending in right cradle position (follower roll in), side cross side (follower roll out), side cross side ending right cradle position (follower roll in), side cross side (follower roll out), 5678 replace left foot right foot close mark time in place for follower under arm turn right back to closed position. To shorten to two roll outs and fit the phrasing, roll out after only two counts of side basic.

12. Man's Circle Wrap 1234 open break and mark time, 5678 continue to mark time leading follower to end in RCradP, six back walks turning left in RCradP ending by rolling partner out facing double hand hold.

13. Progressive Congo (4 Directions) three (side cross side) walks in promenade position and right foot tap in closed position, three (side cross side) walks in closed position and left foot tap in facing position, three forward walks and right foot tap back in Facing position, three walks backward and left foot tap forward.

14. Face Loops starting in facing position, cross hand hold right over left, basic to the side with four leader's face loops, basic to the side with four follower's face loops.

15. Man's Duck Wrap facing position, cross hand hold left over right, 12 open break, 34 left foot side break with partners under arm turn left, 5678 under arm turn right to leader's hammer lock and leader's duck, 1234-mark time for followers under arm turn left, 5678 basic to side with leader's face loops.

Merengue Bronze Variations

1. Cradle Circle (Rumba)
2. Spot Turn Combination (Rumba)
3. Progressive Basic (Cha Cha)
4. Cradle (East Coast Swing)
5. Cradle to Hammerlock (East Coast Swing)
6. Double Face Loop (East Coast Swing)
7. Check and Circular Walk (Bolero)
8. Side Breaks and Cross (Mambo)
9 Promenade Swivel and Close (Mambo)
10 Alternating Underarm Turns (Mambo)

Merengue Silver

16. Crossbody Leads closed position, facing forward rock, left foot side rock (follower 2 forward walks and a pivot), two forward walks, left foot side close.

17. Crossbody Cradle Wheel open facing, double hand hold, left foot side close, left foot side close, cross body lead, left foot forward close (lady under arm turn left to cradle position), 6 back walks turning left (lady 6 forward walks turning L). Like cradle circle in rumba.

18. Alternating Underarm Turns open facing position, double hand hold, 12 left foot back break, 3 left foot side step (lady right foot side step underarm), 45 right foot open break, 6 right foot side step underarm (lady left foot side step), 78 left foot open break. Repeat again. Like she goes, he goes, she goes in hustle.

19. Hip Circle emphasis on the figure 8 action, start in closed with side steps to the left, (lady full under arm turn right and then ½ turn right to end up in position in front of leader), leader taps to match footwork and side steps to the right then back to the left, lead the right shoulder to turn back to facing position with tap to reconcile footwork.

20. Crossbody with Checked Rock closed position, left foot forward rock, left foot side rock (lady 2 forward walks), left foot side rock (lady right foot back rock, pivot), two forward walks.

21. Man's Wrap and Shoulder Wrap open facing position, double hand hold,
The wrap: 12 left foot open break bring right hand over own head while leaving left hand low, 34 left foot forward walk to right foot side step (lady two forward walks around behind man), 5 left foot back, 6 right foot back leading under arm turn right for partner, 78 left foot forward right foot close.
The shoulder wrap: open facing position, double hand hold 12 left foot open break, 3 left foot side step turning right raising both hands (Lady right foot side step), 4 right foot forward check bringing right hand down to own left elbow (lady left foot side step and tap) completing a full turn to the right, left foot back and close (lady right foot forward to quick under arm turn right), left foot side and close.

22. Around the Back Roll Out Spins open facing position, left-to-right hand hold, left foot back open break, left foot side and cross behind changing hands behind the back (lady right foot forward and side step), mark time (lady roll out), left foot back open break, six forward steps turning right (lady 3 under arm turn left), left foot side and close with head loop (lady right foot side and close).

23. Pretzel open facing position, double hand hold, left foot back break, two forward walks turning right with head loop (lady two forward walks), left foot forward to side step turning left (lady two forward walks turning left with head loop), left foot side and close turning left (lady right foot side and forward walk with head loop), left foot forward and close turning right with head loop (lady two forward walks), mark time (lady two forward walks and head loop), left foot side and closes (lady right foot forward and close turning right), left foot side and close.

24. Coffee Grinder closed position, left foot side and close, left foot side and close change to double hand hold, left foot back and hold, right foot forward and hold.

25. Back Spot Underarm and Check with Twists open facing position, left-to-right hand hold, left foot back open break, 4 steps of back spot turn (lady 3 steps an under arm turn right), left foot close and replace (lady right foot forward pivot turn to man's right side), left foot side break (lady right foot side break), spot turn (lady free spin right foot forward and side turning left), side rocks (lady swivels), side rocks (lady swivels).

27. Pass Behind the Back and Face Loop closed position, 12 open break to left-to-right hand hold, 34 hand change behind partner's back now right-to-right hand hold, 5678 continue under arm turn right for partner into shadow position gathering left to left hand hold in addition to right-to-right hand hold, lead partner out from shadow to open break, turning her to pass behind your back by raising your left hand over your head, lead partner from behind your back with left hand, lead turn and face loop to finish.

28. Left and Right Turn Combination double hand hold, open break, to hammerlock, roll partner out of hammerlock to side-by-side position right to left hand hold, then to roll in to cuddle position gathering double hand hold, roll out of wrap position with raising of right hand to give partner two turns to the right starting with a turn lead over leader's head as leader turns, sixteen counts total.

29. Pivots and Dip 1-4 side basic, 56 5th position break, 78 swivels, 1234 pivots turning right, 56 5th position break, 78 left arm up pose, 1234 dip, 56 5th position break, 78 side together.

30. Back Spot Turn Combination closed position 12 open break, 34 back spot turn turning left, 56 lead IS under arm turn right for partner, 78 gather partner to continue spot turn, 12 OS under arm turn right for partner, 45 gather partner, 56 partner out to right, right to left hand hold fan position, 78 roll partner in while turning, 1-8 swivels.

31. Fallaway turning Swivels (not syllabus) Lead partner back for a rock step while also doing a rock step, replace from rock step, turn 180 to the right and step, then close. Repeat to get a full 360 turn.

Bachata

The rhythm for Bachata is three steps and a tap, 1234 with only a tap on 4, no step. The tap is replaced by a hip lift or a hip and knee lift for advanced dancers. The hip lift is accomplished by tapping with the toe and straightening the leg to push the hip up and tightening the muscles between the shoulder and the hip to lift the hip up. In the description of the figures, tap is used to describe what could be a tap or a hip lift. The steps in Bachata are done using Cuban action to roll the hips in a figure *8 keeping the knees flexed to make a smooth rolling motion with the hips*. The most similar dance is probably Merengue, even though most Merengue figures step on every beat, Merengue does have some 123 tap figures.

Many of the figures are danced in closed position, but can also be done in open or double hand hold. The closed position is right front to right front so that each partner's right foot can step between partner's feet and legs. Bachata is commonly danced in a hold that is connected at the waist and side. Shoulders are given space to create separate added movement. The connection can wrap around partner more than most dance holds if a closer hold is desired.

Bachata Figures

1. Stationary Basic left foot slightly side, replace weight to right foot, left foot closes to right, tap repeat going to the right.
2. Side to Side Basic left foot to the side, right foot closes to left foot, left foot to the side, tap, repeat going to the right.
2A. Cross Basic left foot to the side and slightly back, right foot crosses over left foot, left foot to the side, tap, and repeat going to the right.
3. Forward & Back Basic left foot forward, right foot forward, left foot forward, tap, repeat going back.
4. Half Pivot side basic to the left, on 5, pivot ½ turn to the right and continue side basic to right.
4A. Half Top Turn, side basic to the left, on 5, hook ½ turn to the tight and continue side basic to right.
5. Half turn with Under Arm Turn is same as 4 with an inside under arm turn on the turn.
6. Left & Right Turns Under arm turns for follower are lead as an outside under arm turn when the man is going left and an inside turn when the man is going right.
7A. Alternating Turns outside turn for lady going left, behind the back for the man going right which changes the hands, outside turn for lady going left in cross hand hold, loop over the head going back to normal hand hold.

7B. Behind the Back This figure could be a reach behind back or a turn for man changing hands behind the back.

8. Walk Around Turn. This is both turn on a side basic.

9. Shadow with Turns while doing a side basic and back make a hand change, from an open break roll partner into shadow position make a foot change by taping or holding a count, move partner from right side to left side and back, make under arm turns while changing sides, roll partner out with a double turn and a foot change.

10. Hammerlock into hammerlock while doing a basic to the left in Double hand hold lead an outside turn keeping hold of both hands, to exit while doing a basic to the right in hammerlock hold lead an inside turn. Add a face loop for flare.

11. Cuddle with Turn while doing a basic left in Double hand hold lead an inside under arm turn keeping both hands. Partner can be moved from side to side during side basics. Exit by reversing the turn back out to Double hand hold.

12. Alternating Turn with Neck Wrap, Double Hand Turns while doing a basic left in Double hand hold lead an outside turn, lead turn opposite direction going right but head loop right hand over lady's head, turn opposite to unwind partner, but put a hand over your head for shoulder wrap, turn opposite to unwind.

13. Man's Behind the Back to Lady's Turn at the beginning of a basic man's left basic, hand to lady's left shoulder for a shoulder turn followed by a man's behind the back turn which get a right-to-right hand hold for a series of wraps and turns.

14. Man's Hammerlock into shadow sweethearts. While side stepping left with right-to-right hand hold, man turns to the left into a man's hammerlock position, man does a turn and a half to the right to unwind from hammerlock ending up behind partner in sweetheart position for series of side to sides with under arm turns. Use a turn and a half to roll partner out of sweetheart position.

15. Bridge Basic left with a 4-count dip rolling from one side to the other.

16. Cuddle to roll outs Start with a Cuddle and roll out to side-by-side position. From this position do roll ins and roll outs. End with a free spin or dip.

Hustle

Hustle timing is &123 &456 &781 and on. &1 in the past was a rock step, now it is danced as a ball change. Although the hustle has 4 steps per figure, the ball change is really just one step so that all of the figures start on the same foot, therefore many of the figures from other dances that have 3 steps per figure (rumba, night club two step, bolero, mambo, salsa, etc.) will work in hustle. Single time swing is also very similar in that the rock step is the same as the ball change in hustle, therefore many of the figures can be adapted either way. Much of hustle is danced in Double Hand hold.

Hustle Bronze Figures
The following breaks are used on the &1 depending on the figure.
A. Back Break is a small step back.
B. Side Break is a step to the side.
C. Forward Break is a step forward

Hustle

1. Hesitation In Double hand hold, & left foot slightly back *on the ball of the foot only*, 1 replace weight on the right foot (these two steps are the ball change), 2 left foot forward, 3 right foot back.
2. The Wheel is the same as the hesitation with up to ½ turn on each &123.
3. Underarm Turn Combination (You Go, I Go, You Go) In Double hand hold, ball change, **She goes:** lead an inside under arm turn for partner with the *left* hand looping over partner's head with a right ½ turn letting go of right hand on the beginning of the turn, trailing the hand around partner's middle back and recapturing the hand with slide under partner's at the end of the turn, partner's back will face leader in the turn and partner will also turn ½ turn in sort of a trading of places. In Double hand hold, ball change, **He goes:** raise *right* hand turning right ½ turn under the arm releasing left hand on the beginning of the turn, partner trails hand across leader's back and recaptures the hand with an arm slide on the end of the turn, leader's back will face follower's front during the turn. Repeat she goes.
4. Leader's Behind the Back Pass and Follower's Bridge From left-to-right hand hold, lead partner forward and step forward, collect follower's right hand with leader's right hand and turn ½ turn to the left and change hands again to complete part 1. Raise the left hand and allow partner to pass underneath turning ½ turn to the right as follower goes to the other side for part 2, ending in open position.

5A. Cross-Body Lead From closed position, side break to the left then ½ turn to the left staying in closed position.

5B. Cross-Body Lead with Open Break to Return From closed position, cross body-lead to open position for part 1, returning to closed position for part 2.

6. Return to Face Loop, From Double hand hold, raise right hand to loop around follower's face keeping hold with left hand in front of partner to face loop position with leader's right hand on follower's right shoulder for part 1, then raise the left hand and release the right hand to return to open position for part 2.

7. Double Hand Hold Bridges, From Double hand hold, trade places with follower coming down right side, hands are now crossed, now bring partner back to original position along the same side and the hands will uncross.

8. The Whip, from single hand hold, bring partner into closed position on right side with a ½ turn to the right for the first half of the whip then rock step back and come forward leading an inside under arm turn right for partner ending in single hand hold. This figure is very much like a WC Swing whip with inside under arm turn.

9A. Cradle with Continuous Left, From Double hand hold, lead partner into cuddle position by raising left hand and turning partner to the left keeping hold of right hand for the first part, leader does a side break while partner does a back break, then raise the left hand to roll partner back out to single hand hold. This is like # 6 return to face loop with arm around waist instead of shoulder.

9B. Cradle in and Out, Same as 9A only straight in and out

10. Back Spot Turn Open break into closed, then two sets of &123 turning right, then a side break back out to open position to end. Leader hooks on first right foot step and crosses in front for the next two right foot steps.

11. Grapevine From closed position, ball change then two sets of &123 grapevines to the left starts with left foot crossing forward across the right foot, then do cross body lead for ½ turn and two more sets of grapevines back to starting point.

12. Sliding Doors From a single hand hold, lead partner to pass in front of you going backwards and facing away from you while you are going the other direction dropping hand hold after lead, pickup follower's left hand with your left and lead to pass back to where follower (follower going forward) came from.

13. Cross Body Lead with Inside Turn From closed position, cross body lead with an inside under arm turn on the 23.

14A. Shadow with Comb From single hand hold, spin partner into shadow position changing to left to left hand hold with a big flourish with both partner's arms up and back then lead partner to make a full right turn back out to open single hand hold.

14B. Shadow with Free Spin This figure is the same as 14A) with spin to the right for follower instead of under arm turn.

15. New York Walk From single hand hold, lead partner to walk past using two sets of &123 pointing on the &1 of the second set, when partner gets to the other side walk it back. Think of the figure as an extended change of places.

16. Roll in Roll out starts with an outside underarm turn to side-by-side (loop overhead) then roll in and roll out.

Hustle Variations or Combinations

1. Open Break, Inside Turns, end in Closed Position. Like a She goes, He goes, she goes.
2. Open Break, Double Hand Right Side Pass, Double Outside Turn, end in Closed Position
3. Crossbody Lead with a Follower's Inside Full Turn, Open Break with a Leader's Outside Turn
4. Open Break, Shadow Position, Hammerlock, Right Side Pass, Exchange of Sides in Leader's Hammerlock
5. Open Break, Shadow Position, Reverse Comb, end in Closed Position
6. Syncopated Four-Count Turn
7. Las Vegas to a Sliding Door
8. Open Break, Shadow Position, Inside Half Turn to Comb, Sliding Hand, Push Off Hesitation, End in Closed Position
9. Open Break, Reverse Underarm Turn, Leader's Right Turn, End in Closed Position
10. Open Break, Behind the Back Lollipop Turn (like barrel roll turn in WC, both turn back-to-back, lady first with an extra turn to a rolled-out position), Wrap Turn (has a J hook lead to wrap partner on the way in & releasing for a cross body), End in Closed Position

Night Club Two Step

Night Club Two Step is danced to slow, smooth music. The basic rhythm is 1&2 3&4 or 1a2 3a4. See step two for the basic movement.

Night Club Two Step Bronze

1. Basic Rhythm The basic rhythm is 1&2 3&4 or 1a2 3a4.
2. Two Step Basic 1st half: left foot back, replace weight to right foot, left foot side. 2nd half: right foot back, replace weight to the left foot, right foot side. The basic can be danced in Closed Position or Double Hand Hold.
3. Outside Underarm Turn 1st half of basic, lead under arm turn for partner while taking the back step for the 2nd half of basic.
4. Opening Out Right & Left, left foot back with ¼ turn left while leading partner to turn a ¼ right to side-by-side position still holding frame with the right arm, replace weight to right foot while turning back to closed, left foot side facing partner. Repeat natural opposite on the other side. To exit remain closed after side step.
5. Shadow Position From a right-to-right hand hold on 1&2 lead partner into shadow position on the right side, 3&4 in place, 5&6 move partner to left side, 7&8 lead partner out from shadow. End with a push spin (see figure 14).
6. Flip-Flop outside position in Place 1&2 left foot side break while opening partner out to the right, replace weight to right foot bringing partner back to closed, close left foot to right foot facing partner. Repeat on the other side. Commonly done two opening outs to each side in a set.
7. Shoulder Check From an **open break** (rocking back and coming forward while leading partner to rock back and come forward) lead partner for an inside under arm turn right catching partner on the left shoulder blade with the right hand to stop the rotation at ½ turn, check in front of partner while partner rocks back, lead partner out with an outside under arm turn left to open break position. Figure is commonly repeated a second time.
8. Cradles From Double hand hold, 1&2 lead partner forward raising left hand as in an inside under arm turn right while keeping right hand to end in right side cradle position,3&4 move partner to left side cradle position, 5&6 move back to right side cradle position, 7&8 roll partner back to open position with an outside under arm turn left.
9. Traveling Crosses Left & Right In Double hand hold or closed position move left with side cross side steps (a grapevine). Repeat to the right. Repeat as desired. A change of direction can be made at the end of each side cross side. Also called side crosses.

10. Inside Underarm Turn Lead partner to rock back on 1, then forward for inside under arm turn right on &2, finish with side crosses right on 3&4. Leader rotates ¼ turn to the right while partner is turning.

11. Underarm Turn & Ladies Spin Same as 10) adding an under arm turn on of partner's turn on the traveling cross to the right.

12. Through the Window Right-to-right and left to left hand hold with left hand on top. Open break with left hand over partner's head tuning to face partner, now back with the right hand over the head turning to face partner, now left over partner's head, then traveling crosses with an under arm turn on of the previous turn.

13. Opposition & Travel to the Right left foot side break while partner opens out & comes back then right foot side crosses.

14. Push Spin Open break with left-to-right hand hold, when coming forward leader pushes partner's right hand with leader's right hand to start partner's turn to the to the right, then leader makes a pivot turn to the left.

15. Criss Cross & Underarm Turn Open break leading partner to cross in front of leader facing the same direction as leader with no hand hold after initial lead, partners find left-to-right hand hold after partner has passed across, lead partner to go back to the right and recollect right to left hand hold on the other side (like passes in EC swing), repeat, while partner is passing to the right the second time obtain Double hand hold and do a under arm turn one direction followed by a under arm turn the other direction while holding both hands, end with a side cross to the right.

Night Club Two Step Silver

1. Progressive Flip-Flop outside position with Man's Turn Lead to opening out on right side, side crosses and flip to other side, side crosses flip to other side, end by regaining closed position.

2. Underarm Catch & Opposition Measure 1 Open break to follower's IS under arm turn right,
Measure 2 at the end of the under-arm turn catch partner with right hand while hooking behind and turning to the right ¾ turn, Measure 3 side break or opposition break turning left, Measure 4 end with side crosses.

3. Outside Turn with Man's Hand Change From and open break outside under arm turn for follower while leader hooks for hand change behind the back, lead outside under arm turn for partner, side crosses with under arm turn to finish.

4. Traveling Right Turn Measure 1three forward steps in promenade position, Measure 2 forth step forward and across to cut off partner then hook step and step for 360 right turn, repeat.

5. Shadow Traveler Measure 1R to right hand hold open break to shadow with fake for man (1 2),
Measure 2 back replace forward in shadow
Measure 3 Forward side back, small steps moving partners to left side in shadow
Measure 4 back replace close, setting up for turn of partner
Measure 5 Back walk forward with IS under arm turn for partner to right side shadow
Repeat Measure 2-5 then roll partner to open with hand change and foot fake (1 2)
Open break with OS under-arm turn to finish.

6. Alternating Turns & Around the Back Open break, under arm turn for follower, change to right-to-right hand hold, open break catch partner at the waist and turn right, lead partner around behind the back, ends with side crosses and partner under arm turn.

7. She Goes, He Goes, In Double hand hold, open break and she turns, open break he turns, open break she turns. End by going back to basic. This is like the She Goes, He Goes in hustle.

8. Alternating Rondes' Open break with inside under arm turn, catch partner and hook turning right

9. The Wheel Measure 1 basic, Measure 2 back replace forward with OS under arm turn for partner,
Measure 3 three forward walks turning right, with back of right hand on back of partner's waist
Measure 4 side replace right, bringing hand over head and turning 180 bring partner around behind to end in facing position,

Measure 5 back replace side, bring partner to right side position with loop of right hand over partner's head

Measure 6 Side cross side, turn partner out to facing in X hand Double hand hold

Measure 7 Back replace side, open break with IS under arm turn

Measure 8 Side cross side, continuing under arm turn.

10. Spinning Hammer, Cradle and Corte Open break turn into hammerlock, out of hammerlock into cradle, out of cradle to Corté.

Spot turns
*Nat spot turn, move first to block partner, hook on second step
*Rev spot turn, move partner first, partner hooks

Country Two Step – Bronze

The normal timing for Country Two Step is QQSS, but SQQ and other timings can be used. Movement is normally described as natural walking motion. Country Two Step is a progressive dance like Waltz and Foxtrot however no rise and fall is used.

1. Progressive Basic Forward steps in a basic walking movement, QQSS. (Under arm turns can be lead at the beginning of a QQ or a SS)
2. Promenade Basic Forward steps opening to promenade position
3. Right Turning Basic
a. Half Turn with Natural Finish from promenade position start turn to the right with last slow on prom
b. with Cross Body Lead Ending as above with cross body lead back to Prog
4. Promenade Pivot from promenade position ½ right turn on each slow
5. Left Underarm Turn from Promenade Position from promenade position man closes on second slow and leads left under arm turn on QQ
6. Right Underarm Turn ending in Promenade Position from basic lead turn on QQ
7. Wrap
a. with Walk Out from promenade position, lead inside under arm turn keeping right hand to wrap finish with roll out
b. with Check Turn from promenade position, lead inside under arm turn to wrap, finish with check turn roll out
8. Sweetheart
a. Check Turn with Right Hand roll into shadow on shoulder with hand change turn out with right hand check turn
b. Check Turn with Left Hand roll into shadow on shoulder with hand change turn out with left hand check turn
9. Closed Grapevine from promenade position hook behind on QQ
10. Hand-to-hand Grapevine
a. Hand-to-hand Grapevine Forward from promenade position lead Outside under arm turn into FFBB
b. Hand-to-hand Grapevine Backward from promenade position lead inside under arm turn into FFBB
11. Basket Whip from Basic from a basic, open break by backing up on second slow while partner continues back, then basket whip as in WCS
12. Shoulder Catch lead an OS under arm turn, catch the shoulder and reverse to an inside under arm turn
13. Inside Weave from promenade position IS under arm turn to a Waltz two-way under arm turn

14a. Outside Weave from promenade position OS under arm turn to a Waltz two-way under arm turn
14b. Outside-inside Weave combines the inside and outside weaves
15. Side-by-side free Spins from promenade position outside under arm turn into FFBB with free spins

Country Two Step – Silver

1a. Twist Turn from promenade position like Tango
1b. Twist Turn with Barrel Roll as 1a with both turn (barrel roll) ending
2a. Left Right Check Turn from promenade position OS under-arm turn with hand change to shadow, then turns from shadow
2b. Windshield Wiper from promenade position IS under arm turn with hand change to shadow
2c. Shoulder Roll from promenade position to shadow then duck partner
3. Elbow Catch Free Spin from promenade position FFBB then catch partner's elbow for free spin
4. Wrap in Wrap out from promenade position outside under arm turn to FFBB then roll in roll out
5. Double free Spin from promenade position outside under arm turn to FFBB then both do double turns on QQQQ
6. Right Barrel Roll from promenade position outside shoulder catch, to inside under arm turn to both turn
7. Patty Cake from promenade position inside turn into patty cakes (touching opposite hands) with turns
8. Bow Tie from promenade position inside turns, then right turn into shadow turns
9. Closed Whips from open break, WCS whips IS OS and behind the back
10. Arm Checks inside turns followed by arm checks (girl facing line of dance with arms out hands by waist for leads to twist)
11. Fan Turn from promenade position inside under arm turn, man's turn with hand changes behind the back
12. Lariat behind the back whip, with two way under arm turns (for double turns use QQQQ)
13. Pretzel OS under arm turn picking up free hand for hammerlock in, out and in again
14. Illusion Turns behind the back whip, followed by illusion turns (QQQQ for doubles)
15. Telespin from promenade position, stop, around, Crossbody pivot of sorts

Polka Bronze

The basic rhythm of Polka is "a 1 2 3 _ a 5 6 7 _ ", where "a" is the hop (up and down) and 1 2 3 is a triple step, the 4 & 8 are held like in Salsa. Polka is a fast-moving dance that is most noted by the hop introduced in 8 below. Polka is commonly danced as a progressive dance.

1. **Basic** Triple left, triple right
2. **Progressive Basic Forward & Back** Triple forward and triple backwards
3. **Turning Basic to the Left** Basic turning left
4. **Turning Basic to the Right** Basic turning right
5. **Promenade** Progressive in promenade position
6. **Promenade with Underarm Turn** Triple to the left leading outside under arm turn on the 2 3 and finished on the 567.
7. **Counter Promenade** Basic in counter promenade position
8. **Advanced Basic (add the hop)** Hop up and down before the 123 & the 567.
9. **Outside Turn** From basic turning left add outside under arm turn on the 567
10. **Inside Turn** From basic turning right add inside under arm turn on the 567
11. **Man's Underarm Turn** after partner's outside under arm turn on 567 add leader's turn on the following 123.
12. **Cradle** Same as Inside turn adding arm slide with right hand as the turn begins capturing and holding right hand while leading the turn with the left hand. This places you in side-by-side wrap position. Reverse the process to unwrap
13. **Chassés Left & Right** 1234567 to left and 1234567 to the right
14. **Heel, Toe Chassés** Left chasses 1234567, 1 right foot heel in, 2 left foot toe in crossing in front of right foot, 3 left foot heel in, 4 left foot toe in crossing in front of right. Finish by right chasses or another figure.

Argentine Tango

The frame in Argentine Tango is relaxed and the partners lean in towards each other. If there is contact, it will be at the top of the body very different from American Tango. Argentine Tango allows forward steps to be either heel leads or ball flat. Timings can be changed to suit the music.

1. Basico – Basic closed position, 1-right foot back, 2-left foot side, 3-right foot forward outside partner, 4-left foot forward with left side lead, 5-right foot closes to left foot, 6-left foot forward, 7-right foot side, 8-left foot closes to right foot. All steps are slows. The steps are numbered so that portions of this figure can be used to describe other figures below.
2A. Cambio de Peso en el Lugar - Weight Changes in Place Take a step forward, change weight three times in place.
2B. Paso al Costado - Side Step Side brush, side brush, side brush, all slows
2C. Cadencia - Rock Step left foot forward, right foot back, side facing side
3. Caminada – Walking 2345 of basic left foot ending behind right foot, 3 walking steps, 345 of basic, 3 walking steps, 678 of basic.
4. Ochos Para Adelante - Forward Ochos 2345 left foot ending behind right foot, 2 figure 8's, 3 walking steps left foot first, 678. All slows.
5. Ochos Para Atrás - Back Ochos This figure introduces cross system of partnership movement where both partners step with the same foot at the same time. Start with position 2 of basic, two back ochos (leader stepping forward while partner does swivel steps (step together turn), two forward steps, then steps 678 to finish.
6. Molinete a la Derecha - Windmill to the Right 2345 of basic, then follower does two grapevine steps around leader who is turning right, a back ocho, two forward steps, then steps 678 to finish.
7. Molinete a la Izquierda - Windmill to the Left 23 of basic, then follower does grapevine steps around leader who is turning left, forward walks, then steps 678 to finish.
8. Basico en el Sistema Cruzado - Cross System Basic closed position, 1-right foot back, 2-left foot side *and close*, 3-left foot forward outside partner (*now in cross system*), 4-right foot forward with left side lead (*now in cross system*), 5-hold while partner does cross (*this reconciles back to basic system*) left foot, 6-left foot forward, 7-right foot side, 8-left foot closes to right foot. All steps are slows. The steps are numbered so that portions of this figure can be used to describe other figures.
9. Caminada Variación - Walking Variation closed position 2 of basic (small step to left and change weight to the right foot), four cross system walks in LEFT

Clarke Fairbrother – Dance Nuggets

OUTSIDE POSITION end by collecting left foot to right foot, 345 of basic, two walks in normal system, 678 of basic.

10. Caminada Con Giro - Walking with Turn 23 of basic, forward walks turning FSBBSF, 345 of basic, two walks forward in line, 678 of basic.

11. Sacada con el Pie Izquierdo - Displacement with the Left foot 2345 of basic crossing right leg behind left at 5 with weight, two forward ochos with displacement of follower's foot (leader puts his left foot between follower's feet on the first ocho lifting it up), two forward walks, 678 of basic.

12. Sacada con el Pie Derecho - Displacement with the Right Foot 2345 of basic crossing right leg behind left at 5 without weight, two forward ochos with displacement of follower's foot (leader puts his right foot between follower's feet on the first ocho lifting it up), two forward walks, 678 of basic.

13. Boleo con Cruzada en Espiral - Boleo with Spiral Cross 2 of basic, lead partner to Boleo (follower with bent knee turns ¼ turn right with left leg extended behind) by turning slightly to the left then reverse partner to original position plus ¼ overturned by turning to the right and back to the left while she makes a spiral cross, two walks, 678 of basic.

14. Parada, Barrida & Pasada con Gancho - Stop, Sweep, and Pass Over with Hook 2 of basic, back ocho with stop at the back of the ocho, leader stops follower's foot, leader sweeps follower's foot, rolls to his right ½ turn and blocks follower's foot, follower then blocks leader's foot, steps over and does a hook between leader's legs, leader completes the ocho, takes two forward steps and finishes with 678 of basic.

15. Parada, Sandwich al Reves & Pasada con Media Luna - Stop, Reverse Sandwich, Pass Over with Half left foot Moon 2 of basic, back Ochoa with stop at the back of the Ochoa, leader stops follower's foot with a reverse sandwich, follower sandwiches leader's foot, sweeps the foot in a half moon, follower then steps over and completes the Ochoa, take two forward steps and finish with 678 of basic.

Dance Routines
American Smooth
Waltz Bronze page 15
B1A box step
B1B box step with underarm turn
B8 reverse turn started F DC
B11 turning twinkle
B13 promenade chasse' (1 2 & 3 timing)
B5 promenade close
B2 progressive basic
B7 face to face back-to-back
B8 two-way underarm turn to end the face to face back-to-back.

Waltz Silver page 20
From the middle of the long side, F DW
S2 Open right turn
B13 Promenade chasse'
S10 Challenge line and Oversway
S8B Hairpin from promenade with spin ending to short side
B8 Reverse turn
B2 Progressive basic with passing feet
S16 Rounders' into corner
S17 Check to Open Fallaway, do the fallaway twice, starts CP F DW
S5 Check & Developé, end with ladies spin on the chasse'
S13 Flip Flops
S11 Pivots end backing LOD with impetus end
S6 Chair & Slip pivot
S1 Open left box, restart with S2 Open right turn

Waltz simple Silver
S1 Open left in CP
S2 open right in CP, heal turn
S6 Chair slip
S3 Open left to OS UAT
Forward to closed position (half open left)
S18 Leader back off the track with inside turn to shadow (man chasses) then natural turn in shadow, forward progressive three step x2 (in shadow), natural turn in shadow, Man chasses, lady free spins out of shadow
S13 Flip flops
S11 Pivots
S6 Chair and slip pivot, restart

Tango Bronze page30
B1A Basic
B8B Reverse Turn with outside swivel QQS QQS QQS
B3B Double Corte QQSS QQSS QQS
B1B Turning basic to promenade
B7 Checked promenade SWWSS&S
B5 Open fan with under arm turn to new LOD SSQQS
B4 Progressive rock steps turn to DC SS QQS QQS QQS
  Tango close to promenade SSQQS New LOD promenade close

Tango Silver page 33, starting on end of the long side;
Walk, walk with UAT to PP F DC of short side
S5 Fallaway ronde (first part only)
B6 Running steps + basic E DC NLOD all curving left
S17 Promenade close F DC
S18 S, S, Viennese cross turning left 56&78 from CP to open fan F W
Roll in partner CP DW (Step back on 1, forward 3 change weight 4)
B3A Corte S back S replace, QQS tango close DW
S10 Swivel fans
B8B Reverse turn (end passing) DW QQS QQS
S17 Promenade close F DC
S18 Viennese cross turning left 56&78& E W
S2 Oversway and Ronde 1-2 challenge line, 3-4 over sway, 5-6 ronde partner, and lead fallaway pivot to left and closed finish.
S8 OSUAT to Shadow (Reverse turn 123 W OST to shadow 4&5678 E DC)
B8A Reverse turns QQS QQS E DW in shadow
2 Spanish hooks in shadow (Envelope straight leg up, in, down) 12 34
S6 Spanish Drags in Shadow 567 lunge hold 8 drag slowly up 1234&
  Lower 5678 point foot out left
B5 Shadow to fan, roll partner across 1-2, replace fan 3-4
Swivel close from fan (5 step, 6 tap, 7 step, back 8 close) End DW NLOD

Social Silver Tango
Basic, Reverse turns with swivel, end in PP
Open fan, trade places twice, end with wrap into shadow
Spanish hooks, chase to Spanish drag, throw out to open fan and slow UAT
Two slows to Viennese crosses, challenge line, over sway
Rondae partner, man's spiral, inside UAT for partner

Foxtrot Bronze, page 39
Starting on the **long side** F DW
B12 Grapevine,
B8 Twinkle open,
Variation 6 from waltz, promenade chasse,
B14 Promenade pivot with promenade close,
B3 Overturned left rock turns,
Short side,
B6 two zig zags,
B2 Prom walk,
B5A promenade walk with underarm turn,
B4 sway step,
B5B sway step with under arm turn,
B3 overturned left rock turn,
long side,
B7 box with under arm turn,
variation 8 from waltz, face to face back-to-back with inside under arm turn with two way under arm turn ending.
Foxtrot Silver, page 45 starting end of long side F DW
S3 Grapevine (SQQ to PP, SQQ turn, BSFSBSFS) on the short side
Variation 8A Chasse with OSUAT start back SQ&Q to DW OLOD
V11 from Waltz, Developé to corner
Variation 8A Chasse with inside UAT to Shadow position SQ&Q
S7B Hairpin in shadow into corner SQQ with shadow impetus DW SQQ
S16 Tossing Grapevine in shadow
Variation 8A Chasses with OS turn end open PP
Waltz S13 three Flip flops
S14 Promenade Pivot with impetus end
S5 Chair & slip
S1 Open Left Box
S2 Open right turn 3mea (twinkle to PP) Impetus end to NLOD
Variation 8 Chasse LOD
S6 1-4 Challenge line, 1-4 Oversway 1-4 end PP
S7B Hairpin from PP Curved feather toward DW ALOD
6 LS Chasse, grapevine, Developé
Variation 8A Chasse with OS UAT towards DC
S3 Forward step to 8 count grapevines,
Crossing step points QQQQ 1-4
WS 5 Developé 5-8
(Restart with Chasse to shadow, tossing grapevine)

Viennese Waltz Bronze page 51
B10 Bow & curtsey
B2 5th position L & R
B2 5th position with underarm turn
B3 Reverse turn
B5 Cross body lead with under arm turn opening out
B6 Hand-to-hand twice
B4 Twinkle to close
B3 two reverse turns
B7A Change step
B8 two natural turns
B7A Change step
B3 reverse turn
B5 Cross body lead to opening out
B8 Change of places & back
B5B Cross body with underarm turn to side-by-side face LOD
B6 Face to Face Back-to-back to 2nd corner, side, side (balance steps) restart
Viennese Waltz Silver page 53
B10 Bow & curtsey (Start on short side F DC), with a pull connection, hesitation RF to left, tap with LF Boto Fogo to Right, partner to shadow, 123 shape, roll out with cantor
B3 Reverse turn
B5B Cross body w/UAT opening out
B9 Trading place with turns
B4 Twinkle to close
B3 Reverse turns (two)
B7A Change step
B8 natural turns (or two)
B7A Change step
Waltz B5 Check & Developé
Chasse with UAT to shadow
B3 1/2 reverse turn
B5B Crossbody to opening out to two hand hold 123
Hesitation (1 hold), invite to develop by step back on L OS partner on left side
Cantor (1, hold 2, 3) inside turn to shadow
Tossing grapevines 4 measures in cantor
2 open 360 natural turns in shadow 4 measures, Running change step (to LSL)
Hesitation throw-out (1 hold at F to F), Explosion line (1 hold, push out to Fan)
B9 Trading places,
Twinkle (or fan close) 1-6 E LOD closed

International Standard

Waltz Bronze page 25
FDW Side left, side right, forward prep step on 3
B13 Natural spin turn (which begins with half of natural turn B2),
B4 Full Reverse turn,
B12 Back whisk,
B6 Promenade chasse' (chasse' from promenade position, 12&3 timing),
B7 Natural hesitation change (starts with half a natural turn),
B16 Basic weave (or rev turning chasse'),
B17 Outside change (all passing feet turning left),
B13 Natural Spin Turn, ending new LOD
B15 Double reverse spin turn turning left (1 2 H), reverse turning chasse',
B17 Outside change OP DW (back, ugly foot, forward),
B9 Forward lock steps,
B13 Natural Spin Turn to DC new LOD,
B15 Reverse Spin Turn,
Restart with B4 reverse turn.

Waltz Silver page 27
Facing DW Side left, side right, prep step forward on 3
B13 Natural Spin Turn
S21 Turning Back Lock, 1&23 to DW
B6 Prom Chasse, (12&3 timing)
B10 Impetus Turn to PP DC
S18 Weave from PP FFBBBF E DC
B6 Prom Chasse (12&3 timing)
B13 Checked Nat Spin Turn 1&23 end w Rev Pivot
B15 Double Rev Spin Turn E DC
S23 Open Telemark to Wing (1 march, march 23) E DW
S25 Drag Hesitation 12H3
B9 Back Lock 12&3
S26 Outside Spin E DW NLOD (123 full turn to right over 3 steps)
Restart

Tango Bronze page 35
Long side
2 walks DC (restart with reverse turn)
B13 Reverse turn (end OSP) QQS QQS
B11 Left foot Rock Step QQS turning 90R w LSL OSP End DWALOD
B2 Closed Promenade
B1 Progressive Link QQ, hold for 1 or 5
B5 Twist turn SQQ SQQ end LOD PP
B7 Natural Promenade Turn SQQS (end PP, NLOD)
Short Side
B2 Closed Promenade SQQS DW
1 walk curving
B4 Progressive side Step Reverse Turn end W
B1 Progressive link QQ ends LOD PP
B7 Natural Promenade turn SQQS DW ends closed
B11 Left foot rock (back on l) QQS rotate right 90
B2 Tango close back QQS turns left to DW
2 Walks SS curving (think of these as basics)
B3 Progressive side step QQS
1 Walk DCNLOD

Foxtrot Bronze page 47
starts on the long side F DC:
Side to the left 1-4, Side to the right 5-7, left foot preparation step DC on 8
B1 RSL CP Feather step SQQ (ends OSP LSL)
B2 Reverse turn, strong LSL SQQ through feather finish SQQ ends OSP LSL
B3 Three step* SQQ, ends CP w strong RSL
B8 RSL Natural weave SQ,QQQ,QQ with Feather finish, ends LSL OSP
B2 ½ rev turn SQQ with a back-step S to DC NLOD
   Short Side
B5 LSL Basic weave 6Q L end LSL OSP as above
B3 Three step* SQQ, to closed RSL on step 2,
B4 Natural turn SQQ and SSS to NLOD

*Three step LF start, H HT TH, SSS ends natural turn
  Starts OSP LSL, ends CP RSL, precedes natural turn

**Feather step RF start H T TH, ends reverse turn
  Starts CP RSL, ends OSP LSL, precedes reverse turn

Foxtrot Silver page 48
starts F DC:
Side to the left 1-4, side to the right 5-7, prep step on 8,
B1 Feather step to DC,
S15 Open Telemark to DW,
B4 Natural Turn to backing LOD,
S17 Open impetus to DC,
S19 Natural Weave from promenade DW (6Q's),
S19 Three step to DW, hover cross (1S 6Q) to DC NLOD,
S20 Closed Telemark to DW,
B1 Feather step for OSP ends OSP DW,
B6 Reverse wave SQQ SQQ to backing LOD,
S17 Open impetus DC new LOD.

Clarke Fairbrother – Dance Nuggets

Quick Step page 57
Side 1
Prep step DW
B8 Natural spin turn RSL SSS, Back, side, close LSL SQQ
B4 ½ rev turn SQQ,
B2 Progressive chasse, SQQS end OSP
B3 Forward lock OSP SQQS towards DW
B4 ½ Nat SQQ w back locks OSP SQQS BLOD E OSP
B7 Running finish SS to turn S to DWNLOD E OSP
Side 2
B4 ½ Nat SQQ
B6 back locks OSP SQQS E OSP
B10 Tipple Chasse, Chase SQQS, Forward lock QQS, End DW new LOD OSP

American Rhythm

Cha Cha Bronze American or International page 70
B2 Basic
B5 Cross over breaks, left and right
B15 Cross over flick, Cross over and flick
B5 Cross over break,
B14 Three Cha Chas, forward and back locks
International B14 Natural top from and open break
International B16 Closed Hip twist
B6 Cross body to
International B9 Time Steps
B5 Cross body lead to
B14 Three Cha Cha's (Locks back and forward)
B10 Shadow Positions (from cross hand position)
B9 Shoulder check
B12 Alternating UATs
B4 Outside partner
B3 Progressive basic

Cha Cha Silver American or International page 72
B1 Basic using forward and back locks
International B12 Check to right side pass (Hockey Stick)
S1 Crossover Break with flick
B15 Crossover and flick with spiral turn
B7 Open Break to International B14 Natural Top
International B16 Closed hip twist
B6 Cross body with UAT
International B9 Time Steps
B13 Cross Body Pull Back
International B6 Check to Turn, check to back locks
S11 Check to Turkish towel
B10 Shadow Cross Body Leads with UATs
S2 Back spot turn with quick UAT
S3 Pull back grapevine
S4 Cross body, surprise, quick turn
S10 syncopated cross over variations

American Rumba Bronze page 78
B14 Circular walks with inside UATs
B6 Slow UAT to back basic
B13 Quick UAT, face loop & UAT
B5 Open Break with UAT
B4 Cross body,
B8 Cross over breaks
B9 Cross over and sit, tap, turn
B11 Open break, Shoulder checks with Double UAT,
B1 Time steps
B4 Cross body (restart)
B2 5th position
B5 Outside partner, Like Cha Cha Shoulder to shoulder
B9 Cross over and side rocks
B12 Cradle circle, hand-to-hand
B15 Spot turns

American Rumba Silver page 82
B3 Box, Back ½ of Box, forward S B1 QQ cucaracha to R
B1 or cucaracha to the left with UAT, S close
B1 QQS to R,
B4 Cross Body Lead using QQ alternate forward check for the L side pass
International B11 Fan or Open Break to R side pass
International B13 Hockey stick
International B16 back walks to opening outs
V12 Crab walks
V13 Pivot
International B3 Cucarachas
International B6 or B11 Shoulder to shoulder
S8 Lady Swivels
B10 Open break to side-by-side
B14 Open Circular Walks w UATs
Back walks to open break
B12 Cradle Circle with roll in roll out
B 13 Quick UAT, face loop and curl

International Rumba Silver page 84
B1 Open basic
B11 Fan
B 13Hockey Stick
B1 Open basic
Two back rumba walks
B15 Block for natural top
B16 Opening outs
S23 Spiral turn (stand in place)
B11 Fan
B12 Alamena
S25 Rope spin (lead down & around, step back, step side)
Walk around
B4 New Yorker
S22 Aida
Restart

East Coast Swing Bronze page 88
B3 Shoulder roll
B6 Double OS UAT
Jive B8 Hip bumps
S6 Passes
B5 IS UAT
B7 American spin
Jive G25 Toe heal swivels
Jive B13 2 Whips and throw out
J G 29 Back walk & kicks
Progressive with hip twists
B9 Shoulder Checks
B16 Helicopter (hand change)
B11 Cradle to hammerlock

East Coast Swing Silver page 90
B3 Basic Turning left
B6 Under arm turn out for partner JB8 Hip bump
S11 Progressive closed series w kickball changes
S12 Chasse pivots 4 counts
S13 Pivots 4 counts
JS 21 Throwaway fall away, points, Kick ball changes
S9 Trading places turn
S8 Drunken sailor to hip thrusts
SJ 19 Simple Spin section, drunken sailors with Rock out on 78
S9 Trading places turn into progressive open series
S 14 Pivot Whip
S 13 Hook Whip
JS 29 Miami Special from R to R hand hold
S7 Boogie Walks
B3 Basic turning
JS 18 Roll off the arm (cradle with roll out)
JB 7 Change or hands behind back
B6 Rock into double UAT for restart

Bolero Silver page 96
B1 Basic turning L,
S9 Crossover, Quick sit, Rumba rock
S4 Curl, fan, lunge (Same foot lunge)
B7 Romantic sway
B5 Crossover breaks
B2 Open Break and Underarm Turn with hand change
V 11 5th position breaks
B3 Underarm pass UAT (double)
One leg sit open break
B8 Check & under arm pass
S2 Over turned cross body (handshake hold)

Mambo and Salsa page 101
B1 Basic
S10 Two Jazz boxes (four measures), cucaracha while opening partner
S11 Two back Cuban breaks,
S12 crab walk
S3 Bobby's Break
B11 Crossbody Lead w UAT
B7 Two shoulder checks (Peak a boos)
B5 Spiral turn and a three step turn for partner
B15 Cross over and foot Swivels
B10 Rueda basic
S13 Same foot lunge (Foot between the legs)
S6 Mambo Wrap
Right side-pass with hand change and both turn
Cross hand hold to shadow (arm on shoulder) Side step and tap in opposition
S8 Cross over Rueda Basic Extended Cross body lead

Salsa Wrap - Open break, turn with hand change behind the back, basic in R to L HH, forward check with waist lead of cross body with spin, capture in closed hold.

Salsa Social Step – cross body lead to partner in front, opposing side checks, turn partner to face left side pass.

Spiral – cross body lead to cross hand hold, hands over heads, UAT while crossing to partners left.

Wrap to Right, roll in, roll out and dip.

Samba page 106
IS 14 Reverse turn
IB2 Whisks
B7 two forward Samba walks
IS 20 Roll off the arm
B7 forward Sam walks
IS20 Roll off the arm
B7 one forward samba walk
B7 one side samba walk
B8 two Boto Fogos
B13 Voltas to the right SSQQQQ
IB1D Progressive Basic (Right locks in and out)
B13 Left Voltas SSQQQQ
IB1D Left locks in and out
IS 18 Back rocks
IS 15 Corta Jaka end with R tap
V6 Flip flops
Start over into reverse turn

Paso Doble Bronze page 111

1-4	Arms
5-8	B1 Surplace, March starting on R
1-4	B2 appel B7 forward - Deplacement
5-8	B2 appel & B7 forward - Deplacement
1-4	B1 March open to side - surplace
5-8	B4 Side steps back - Chasse to right Promenade
1-4	B5 appel & forward - chasse to left Promenade
5-8	B4 Side steps back - Chasse to right Promenade
1-4	B3 Appel to left
1-16	B15 Sixteen (appel, 2, 3 forward & turn, 4,5,6, 7close, 8-15 in place, tap)
1-4	B13 Fallaway (Rock turn)
5-8	B13 Fallaway (Rock turn)
1-8	B13 Fallaway Ronda pivot
1-8	B17 Grand Circle
1-8	B16 Promenade to counter promenade
1-3	Highlight

Paso Doble Silver page 113

Hands (four counts)
B7 Two displacements (appel {stomp}, forward, side, close)
B4 Chasse 4 counts turning right (on balls of feet)
S23 Coupe de Peak (tap across, close, back, Close, back, close, chasse to right 123456&78)
B16 Promenade to counter promenade (appel, step PP, across in CBMP, Block lady, 90 to R, 90 to R, forward, forward PP)
Mini highlight (Forward, side, tap)
S24 Left foot variation (123, 4 tap behind, &5 R close & L to side, close, R, close)
S22 Fall away ronde' to reverse pivot (123 turn to back LOD, ronde, rev pivot)
B17 Grand circle (Step forward, hold split weight while partner Walks around, big lunge to right on 678)
B16 Promenade to counter promenade (appel, step PP, across in CBMP, Block lady, 90 to R, 90 to R, for, for PP)
S25 Spanish line (taps) Ieta to Spanish line,
S26 Flamenco taps
Highlight
Restart

Night Club Dances

West Coast Swing Bronze page 114
B7 Starter, Throw out
B13 Sugar push
B13 Sugar push face loop with push off to drunken sailor from EC
B4 Right side pass
B9 Whip with turns,
B14 Basket whip
B2 Left Side Pass,
B15 Continuous whip
B7 Half whip to closed, Start again

West Coast Swing Silver page 116
S8 Syncopated sugar push
S2 Rollin & pass (step, replace, step back on 3)
S6 Spinning hammer lock (step, close, tap on 3)
S1 Checked whip & throw out
S2 Rollin & pass
S3 Double face loop & tuck spin
S4 Man's Hammer Lock with Tummy whip
S5 Lock whip, Side Break and Spin
S11 Hammer lock tuck from sugar push
S12 Swivel walks from hammer lock
S13 Hustle whip with shoulder roll
S14 Cha Cha Step
B8 Whip with behind the back-hand change to Sailor Shuffles with head loop

Merengue Bronze page 122
B1 Basic w UATs
B3 Side breaks
B11 Roll out roll in (hand change on 2)
B14 Face loops 1-4
B8 Merengue slide 5-8

Merengue Silver page 124
S29 Pivot and Dip (swivels, pivot, open out, dip) Cucaracha on 3 4
S17 Cross body w UAT to cradle w walk around
S31 Fall away turning swivels
B7 Two Simple Congas (PP SS, close & back, toe up)
B7 Turning Conga (Step turn Step tap), just partner, both, both, just partner
B10 Left spot turn w IUAT partner (1)

Bachata page 127
4 Basic with pivot turns
5 Basic with top turns
6 Outside & inside turns
7 alternating turns
8 Walk around turn
9 Shadow with ladies turns, hand change, open break, to shadow with tap
10 Hammerlock with face loop
11 Cradle with side to side
12 Alternating turns with neck wrap (2 hand turns)
13 Man's wrap
14 Man's hammerlock into sweetheart Hand on shoulder
16 Cuddle to rollouts to dip

Hustle page 129
B1 Hesitation
B5B Cross body out, roll back in
B13 Cross body with UAT
B4 Behind back pass
B2 Wheels
B3 Alternating Loop turns (He goes She goes)
B16 Roll in Roll out
B11 Grapevine (side travel basic)
B14 Shadow turns
B14A Shadow with comb
B14B Shadow with free spin
B9 Cradle in and out
B12 Sliding doors passes

Night Club Two Step Bronze page 132
B2 Basic
B9 Left turns with crosses
B13 Opposition and travel to the right
B8 Cradle w/hand change
B6 Flip flops
B5 Shadow
B7 Shoulder check
B14 Push spin
B12 Through the window

Night Club Two Step Silver page 134
B3 Basic to outside UAT
S2 Underarm catch & opposition from open break, (Bobby's break).
S3 Outside turn then man's hand change turn
S5 shadow traveler with 90-degree angles
S9 the wheel (rope spin)
S10 Spinning hammerlock, cradle & Corté
S4 traveling right (pivots in PP)
S10 spinning hammerlock, cradle & Corte dip
S1 progressive flip flop with man's turn

Country Two Step Bronze page 136
B3 Half turns with natural or cross body exit
B4 Promenade pivots
B7 Wraps
B8 Sweetheart (shadow on the shoulders)
B9 Grape vines, closed and B10 hand-to-hand
B11 Whips open up on the second slow then WCS
B 13 Weaves like Waltz two-way UATs
B15 Side-by-side free spins like waltz FFBB

Abbreviations, 8
Argentine Tango, 139
Bachata, 127
Bolero, 96
Cha Cha, 67
Chassé, 68
Country Two Step, 136
Cuban Break, 77
Cuban Motion, 64
Cucarachas, 67
East Coast Swing, 87
Foxtrot, 39
Hustle, 129
Jive, 93

Mambo, 101
Merengue, 122
Night Club Two Step, 132
Paso Doble, 111
Peabody, 60
Polka, 138
Quick Step, 57
Rumba, 78
Samba, 106
Spot turns, 135
Tango, 29
Viennese Waltz, 51
Waltz, 16
West Coast Swing, 114

Made in the USA
Columbia, SC
25 June 2023